The Confessions of a Baptist Preacher

by John Osteen

ISBN 0-912631-00-7

Lakewood Church
P.O. Box 23297
Houston, Texas 77228-3297

Contents

Contents

Introduction

I have written this book to help God's people everywhere. It will help you to know exactly how to confess the Word of God and experience great changes in your life.

This book is intended to be used as a guide in confessing God's Word. It is not to be used and laid aside. Keep it available at all times. Use these scriptural confessions so much that they become your very own. It may seem awkward at first, but if you will faithfully continue on a daily basis to confess God's Word, not only will you be changed, but your circumstances will change.

We, as Christians, are engaged in spiritual warfare! *For we wrestle not against flesh and blood, but against principalities, against powers, against the rulers of the darkness of this world, against spiritual wickedness in high places* (Ephesians 6:12).

God, through Jesus Christ, has totally defeated Satan. *Now thanks be unto God, which always causeth us to triumph in Christ, and maketh manifest the savour of his knowledge by us in every place* (2 Corinthians 2:14)

God has left to us the responsibility of enforcing that victory, and He has given us spiritual weapons. *For the weapons of our warfare are not carnal, but mighty through God to the pulling down of strong holds; casting down imaginations, and every high thing that exalteth itself against the knowledge of God, and bringing into captivity every thought to the obedience of Christ* (2 Corinthians 10:4-5).

God's Word is a powerful weapon. This book will teach you how to use that weapon. Life has many conflicts, but as we learn to use His Word, we will drive the devil from the field of battle!

We are this day what we have been continually saying with our mouths in days past. If you want to change, you must first change your thoughts. Then, in turn, you will change what you say with your mouth.

In this book I have written some of the most intimate and effective ways I pray and confess God's Word daily. Many times I do not feel or see things as I desire them to be, but I keep on confessing what God has to say about the situation, and these things leap into reality.

Most of us want to get out of a conflict in the quickest and easiest way possible. You may say, "Brother Osteen, what is a conflict?" A conflict is a prolonged battle or struggle. For many, life seems to be a continual struggle. This book is written for those people.

The changes in our lives may not come instantly. Deliverance often comes to us gradually.

You must see yourself as God sees you

Confess God's Word daily until the visual image you have of yourself has changed to match the truth of God's Word. As you boldly make these confessions that we have set forth for you, you will begin to see yourself:

- well instead of sick
- victorious instead of defeated
- joyous instead of depressed
- set free instead of bound!

Let me strongly state that this book has nothing to do with mind over matter or positive thinking as such. We are dealing with the great eternal promises and laws of God.

When you believe God's Word in your heart and confess it with your mouth, GOD STANDS BEHIND YOU TO MAKE IT GOOD IN YOUR LIFE! *For verily I say unto you, That whosoever shall say unto this mountain, Be thou removed, and be thou cast into the sea; and shall not doubt in his heart, but shall believe that those things which he saith shall come to pass; he shall have whatsoever he saith* (Mark 11:23).

This book will help you to speak and to have the desires of your heart. I have found that only God's Word can reveal the desires of my own heart.

Confession is not just a theory

The principles set forth in this book have been tried in the crucible of my own life! I remember when we were told that our own baby daughter had brain damage. The doctor said she would never be normal. She had no sucking reflexes, no muscle tone, and all the other symptoms of cerebral palsy. Through faith in Jesus and confession of His Word, she was healed. She is now grown and has been perfectly normal ever since the Lord Jesus made her whole. There is not one trace of her former condition.

My heart reaches out to other little boys and girls who need the same experience that Lisa had. They need their bodies to be touched with God's healing power. This healing power comes as we confess His Word.

I remember the time when my nervous system collapsed, and I was attacked with a sense of purposelessness. I lost all sense of direction and initiative. I felt that life held no hope or reality. When day came, I wished for night. When night came, I wished for day. I was assaulted by demon powers with such fear that God was no longer real to me. Sleep would not come, and I would lie awake night after night in mental torment from the presence of demonic forces.

God delivered me from that condition. He totally healed me, not instantly, but completely! It was through the confession of God's Word that victory came.

My heart is burdened for the masses of people living in mental torment. They too can be healed! Through the Word of God I was able to climb out of that dark hole of fear. My desire is to help you learn to confess God's Word and do the same.

Some years later I went through a period of pain in my back and legs. This continued for months until I could do nothing but cry out in agony. I faced back surgery and had visions of being paralyzed and unable to walk. Jesus completely healed me without surgery.

I am not against surgery, doctors, medication, or anything else that can help mankind. I just thank God that I was healed through the confession of God's Word.

Another battle came in March of 1974. I lay in Methodist Hospital, awaiting open-heart surgery. Thank God, I did not have to have it. The Lord Jesus permeated my whole being with faith and assurance as I read and confessed His Word!

These are incidents from my own life, which have taken place over a period of many years. Not only in my life, however, have we seen God's Word work. Through the years, we have received countless letters from others who have found that God's Word, spoken by the mouth of the believer, produces health, life, and victory.

Even as I write these words and bring back these experiences to my mind, my heart is flooded with love for one Person: HIS NAME IS JESUS!

Jesus is indeed the same yesterday, today, and forever (see Hebrews 13:8). What Jesus was yesterday, He is today, and He will be forever. What Jesus said yesterday, He is saying today, and He will be saying forever. What Jesus did yesterday, He is doing today, and He will be doing forever. Jesus came to earth to reveal the great love of God, our Heavenly Father.

The Lord Jesus delivered me and my family out of all these conflicts and many more. He did not do it instantly, but He did it! This book will help you change your circumstances. Your present conflict, your field of battle, can become your greatest victory ground!

Many people receive instantaneous miracles, but most people do not. Do not be discouraged if your change comes slowly. When you have discovered what God wants you to know—and understand the principles presented to you in this book—YOU WILL WIN ALL THE BATTLES OF LIFE!

You will come to KNOW that the Lord Jesus is always available to YOU. You will not have to find someone you feel is special to pray for you. You are very special to your Heavenly Father, and He will listen to YOU!

You are loved!

Finally, let me say, I have written this book because I love you. I may not even know you, but I love you. My heart reaches out to you who are suffering in your spirit, mind, and body. I reach out to those of you who have family problems and financial needs. You may be living in disappointment—bruised and brokenhearted by conflicts in your life. Perhaps you carry an unbearable load of guilt. I am reaching out to you.

I could wish for arms long enough to reach around all the human race and lift it up to see and to feel the great love of God in Christ Jesus. I know that what I feel is the compassion of Jesus in me reaching out to you.

JESUS LOVES YOU! Open your heart to Him right now, and invite Him into your life as Savior and Lord. Trust the Holy Spirit to be your Teacher.

Please do not give up! God's Word works. Read this book again and again, and use it as a textbook and manual for confession. It is sent forth in love and in the Name that is above every name, JESUS!

GOD'S THOUGHTS WILL BECOME YOUR THOUGHTS, AND GOD'S WORDS WILL BE-COME YOUR WORDS.

1

The Sound of the Name of Jesus

This is a great day to be alive!

It will be recorded in history that ours has been one of the most turbulent, violent, and shocking generations that has ever lived upon the face of this earth. The truth of the matter is that untold legions of demonic forces have been unleashed upon humanity in these closing days before Jesus comes again.

We have seen youth, driven to every kind of excess, march into our streets like a murky, seething river of pollution. Across the nation, colleges, universities, and lower schools have been rocked by rebellion. Not finding help in traditional religion, and being unable to cope with the powerful and evil spiritual forces arrayed against their minds, these young people have given up, gone under, broken down, and many times committed suicide!

I have conducted their funerals! I have faced the stark reality of the tragedies wrought upon the precious children of our day. I have walked among them on the streets and in the packed wards of mental institutions.

Adult society feels the power of this demonic assault. Alcoholism, drugs, nervous breakdowns, divorce, mental illness, crowded hospitals, prisons, and psychiatric wards demonstrate the hopelessness of mankind. Nakedness, profanity, and bold defiance of every good and noble thing we hold dear has arisen like a giant to challenge us. Men and women filled with demonic power are determined to destroy our heritage—our trust in God—through which our nation was founded. The devil would like to see our foundation crumble. He would like to destroy our trust in God.

There has been a loss of faith in government, the monetary system, educational institutions, and the basic structures which have held us together.

Where is our God? Where is the God of America? Where is the God of the nations of the world? Where is the God of our forefathers? Where is the mighty Savior of our grandparents? Where is Jesus?

Tradition whines sickeningly, "The days of miracles are past." Religion cries, "Divine healing is not for today." Christianity, comfortably settled behind stained glass windows, assures us that demon forces are not real, but only a figment of our imagination.

We who believe on the Lord Jesus Christ, boldly declare before God, the Father of our Lord Jesus

Christ, Jesus Christ, our Lord and Savior, the magnificent Holy Spirit, a great cloud of witnesses, the mighty angels of God, the principalities and powers, the rulers of the darkness of this world, spiritual wickedness in high places, and all the demonic forces stationed on the earth: THE DAY OF MIRACLES IS NOT PAST!

Divine healing for the spirit, mind, and body is available to all! We are not ignorant! We discern the times in which we live, and we know that demonic forces are very real.

Has God forgotten to be gracious? Has Jesus forsaken us? No, a thousand times NO! The Mighty Miracle Worker, the Compassionate Jesus, the Redeemer of all Mankind, has manifested himself with a mighty outpouring of His Holy Spirit.

While the turbulence roars, JESUS walks into our midst. His great power and His great love cannot be hidden. Out of the midst of that murky, profane river of lost humanity, there began to be heard a Name; first on the lips of one, then two, then two hundred, and then thousands...the Name of JESUS. They beheld Him and experienced His love and His transforming power.

Jesus, Jesus, Jesus!

What a sound! Through the BLOOD OF JESUS shed on Calvary, demonic power is broken. Captives are set free by the Name of Jesus.

Today, many of those same youthful rebels are now marching with Jesus. Many people who were broken by divorce, mental oppression, and hopelessness in the past, have been healed in spirit, mind, and body. They are in the forefront with the message of hope. Churches of every denomination and all of society have acknowledged His presence. Jesus is baptizing people in His Holy Spirit and awakening them to the SPIRTUAL POWER He has made available to them.

God will not do the work for us. He has given us great weapons: the Holy Spirit, the Name of Jesus, the blood of Jesus, the Word of God.

God intends for us to take our places as His sons and daughters. He wants us to develop ourselves spiritually. In the mighty Name of Jesus, God has given us power to drive the enemy from us—to defeat the devil and stand tall.

The outpouring of the Holy Spirit has produced BELIEVERS on the earth. Jesus said in Mark 16:17-18, *And these signs shall follow them that BELIEVE; In my name shall they cast out devils; they shall speak with new tongues; they shall take up serpents* (drive out demonic forces); *and if they drink any deadly thing, it shall not hurt them; they shall lay hands on the sick, and they shall recover.*

These believers have taken off their religious masks. They choose to be real! They worship God with their hands lifted high in surrender to Him. They feel the ecstasy of the supernatural, based upon the Bible and its redemptive truths. THEY CARE ABOUT HUMANITY!

You will find these believers inside almost every kind of church. They may be called Catholics, Methodists, Presbyterians, Baptists, Lutherans, Greek Orthodox, Pentecostals, or by many other names.

They are coming together, flowing as a mighty river, and through them God is bringing healing to the nations. Thank God, He has placed within us a river of living water. *In the last day, that great day of the feast, Jesus stood and cried, saying, If any man thirst, let him come unto me, and drink. He that believeth on me, as the scripture hath said, out of his belly shall flow rivers of living water* (John 7:37-38).

We, as individuals, are not perfect. We make mistakes, but we are being changed. Christ is being formed in us! (See Galatians 4:19.) We are moving swiftly toward the end of time. Soon we will step out of time into eternity.

God has set in the church apostles, prophets, evangelists, pastors, and teachers to bring His people into their rightful place of authority. He is teaching us how to defeat the enemy in our individual lives.

God's servants have been faithfully teaching and training believers throughout the last several years. Because of their faithfulness to the task and the eagerness to learn on the part of God's people, there is being heard a sound, THE SOUND OF THE NAME OF JESUS!

The sound of discord, anguish, heartache, confusion, evil, and all sorts of violence, which have dominated the scene and come continually into our ears, are giving way to a new sound, THE SOUND OF THE NAME OF JESUS!

> *But without faith it is impossible to please him: for he that cometh to God must believe that he is, and that he is a rewarder of them that diligently seek him* (Hebrews 11:6).

We are not without faith!

> *…God hath dealt to every man the measure of faith* (Romans 12:3b).

> *Looking unto Jesus the author and finisher of our faith…* (Hebrews 12:2a).

> *So then faith cometh by hearing, and hearing by the word of God* (Romans 10:17).

We know that without faith we cannot please God. We know that God has dealt to each of us the measure of faith. We know that Jesus is the author and finisher of our faith. We know that our faith will grow as we hear the Word of God.

> *And his name through faith in his name hath made this man strong, whom ye see and know: yea, the faith which is by him hath given him this perfect soundness in the presence of you all* (Acts 3:16).

When we take the time to hear the Word of God, that Word will produce in us a steady growth of faith. We will have faith in that Name, and soon we will begin to see as they saw. We will see perfect soundness in our bodies.

We always speak out of the abundance of our hearts. Jesus said that a man will bring forth good things out of the good treasure in his heart (see Matthew 12:34-35).

We are learning to hear God's Word and to hide it in our hearts. We speak God's Word out of our hearts instead of speaking what we see and feel. This Word of God that is hidden in our hearts and spoken out of our mouths will move mountains in our lives!

We no longer are struggling, but we are taking our place in the Body of Christ as mature soldiers. We stand confidently, boldly, and unflinchingly in the face of demon forces. We not only refuse to give in to the attacks of Satan on our spirits, minds, and bodies, but we take the offensive and rescue those around us who have been overcome by the enemy. We do this *in the Name of Jesus!*

We can be heard everywhere speaking and confessing the promises of God. This is the sound of His Name.

The sound of the Name of Jesus!

What a refreshing sound it is. We know that we will rise no higher, nor sink lower than our confession.

> *Wherefore God also hath highly exalted him, and given him a name which is above every name: that at the name of Jesus every knee should bow, of things in heaven, and things in earth, and things under the earth; and that every tongue should confess that Jesus Christ is Lord, to the glory of God the Father* (Philippians 2:9-11).

The Name of Jesus is above every name! When our words have become His Words, every evil force around us must bow to that Name. He has given us the authority to use His Name.

This book is written to help you. Stop speaking the sound of fear. Stop speaking the sound of depression. Stop speaking the sound of sickness and defeat.

Make the decision to live your life full of the blessings of God, full of His joy, and full of His peace.

Put on your lips the sound of the NAME OF JESUS!

2

The Story of a Certain Christian

There was a certain Christian who said he could not—and doubt rose like a giant and conquered him. He talked of failure—and failure became his lot. He spoke continually of sickness—and sickness plagued him. He confessed weakness—and he became weaker.

He told all of his friends and family that debts could never be paid and that he would never have enough money to make it—and poverty moved in to live with him.

He constantly expressed his fear of the past, present, and future—and fear gripped him. He confessed that his marriage was bad and that his children were going to the dogs—and things became worse in his household.

He scattered his words everywhere and, like seeds of poison, they grew around him. To hear him talk, he had it very bad. He thought God was mean to him. HE DID NOT REALIZE HE WAS TO BLAME.

He did not know that he, like God, created things with words. It never occurred to him that mankind is the only creation of God that can speak words from thought and imagination, and thus be a creator like his Maker.

One day this Christian found the truth contained in this book. What is that truth?

> *Death and life are in the power of the tongue: and they that love it shall eat the fruit thereof* (Proverbs 18:21).

> *Thou art snared with the words of thy mouth, thou are taken with the words of thy mouth* (Proverbs 6:2).

> *For verily I say unto you, That whosoever shall say unto this mountain, Be thou removed, and be thou cast into the sea; and shall not doubt in his heart, but shall believe that those things which he said shall come to pass; he shall have whatsoever he saith* (Mark 11:23).

This Christian was amazed at the discovery of a spiritual law. A person creates and brings to pass what he continually says. This law, he discovered, works for good or for bad. He knew it had worked for bad—his whole life proved it. He realized that his words had to change. If his life was going to be different, he knew his words had to be different.

WHAT DID THIS CHRISTIAN DO? He began to read his Bible and see the great redemptive truths therein. He began to understand the reason for and the benefits of the death, burial, and resurrection of Jesus. He began to see himself as God sees him.

GOD LOOKED AT HIM AND SAID:

You are My child.

You are born again of the incorruptible seed of the Word of God.

You are forgiven of all sin and washed in the blood of Jesus.

You are a new creature—delivered from the power of darkness and translated into My kingdom.

You are redeemed from the curse of the law.

You are blessed and healed by My stripes.

You are strong in the Lord.

You are more than a conqueror.

You are the light of the world and the salt of the earth.

You are the righteousness of God in Christ Jesus. Greater is He that is in you than he that is in the world.

You have received the power of the Holy Ghost.

You have power to lay hands on the sick and see them recover.

You have power to cast out devils in the Name of Jesus.

You have power over all the power of the enemy.

You can do all things. The works that I do shall you do, and greater works.

You are My ambassador on the earth to tell every creature the Good News.

I am with you and will never leave you nor forsake you.

This Christian made a great change!

He immediately began to say what God said about him. His words changed, and he boldly confessed to God and to man what God said about him. He said it in the face of demons, circumstances, troubles, fear, and doubt.

HE CONTINUALLY SAID:

I am God's child, for I am born of the incorruptible seed of the Word of God.

I am a new creature—delivered from the power of darkness and translated into the kingdom of God.

I am redeemed from the curse of the law.

I am blessed and healed by the stripes of Jesus.

I am strong in the Lord.

I am more than a conqueror.

I am the salt of the earth.

I am the righteousness of God in Christ Jesus.

I have the Greater One inside me.

I have received the power of the Holy Ghost.

I have power to lay hands on the sick and see them recover.

I have power to cast out devils in the Name of Jesus.

I have power over all the power of the enemy.

I can do all things through Christ who strengthens me.

I am the ambassador of Jesus Christ to tell the GOOD NEWS!

I know that God will never leave me nor forsake me.

At first this Christian made these statements of fact very quietly and timidly. Later he began to believe in his heart what he said with his mouth, and his confession became bold and filled with authority.

His friends thought he was foolish. They even felt he was not telling the truth because things did not look any different. They could not see the evidence of his confession. But this Christian KNEW that he had God's eternal, miracle-working power in his mouth. He KNEW that, according to Hebrews 4:12, God's Word is quick and powerful! He KNEW that God's Word, spoken out of his mouth, would create the changes he so desperately needed in his life. So he believed in his heart and continually confessed the Word of God with his mouth.

> *This book of the law shall not depart out of thy mouth; but thou shalt meditate therein day and night, that thou mayest observe to do according to all that is written therein: for then thou shalt make thy way prosperous, and then thou shalt have good success* (Joshua 1:8).

What God had spoken to Joshua became a living reality to this Christian! God said to Joshua, "LET NOT MY WORD DEPART OUT OF YOUR MOUTH." *But what saith it? The word is nigh thee, even in thy mouth, and in thy heart: that is, the word of faith, which we preach* (Romans 10:8).

Paul explained to us in his letter to the Romans that the Word of God is very near to us—in our mouths, and in our hearts! Remember the words of Jesus in Mark 11:23, *...whosoever shall SAY unto this mountain Be thou removed...he shall HAVE whatsoever he saith.*

Now things are greatly changed!

It did not happen overnight, but this Christian held fast to his confession. The devil pulled hard to get those words out of his mouth, but the Christian persevered. He knew that God could not lie, and he was determined to partake of all of the blessings of God.

Days and weeks and months went by. Things were the same at first, but they slowly began to change. God's Word began to germinate and to produce.

ONE DAY THIS CERTAIN CHRISTIAN REAL-IZED THAT:

- He had confidence instead of doubt!
- He had success instead of failure!
- He had health instead of sickness!
- He had strength instead of weakness!
- He had faith instead of fear!
- He had victory instead of depression!
- He had joy and happiness instead of despair!

This Christian became a stalwart, courageous soldier of the Lord Jesus Christ. The law of the SPIRIT OF LIFE IN CHRIST JESUS had made him free from the law of sin and death.

This Christian had taken the truths of the Word of God, believed them in his heart, confessed them with his mouth, and like God, created his heart's desire.

3

Seven Things We Have in Christ

Let us never be removed from the simplicity that is in Christ! *But I fear, lest by any means, as the serpent beguiled Eve through his subtlety, so your minds should be corrupted from the simplicity that is in Christ* (2 Corinthians 11:3).

Certainly we are to mature in our walk with the Lord. But the more mature we become, the more we exhibit the simplicity of Jesus. We can become so mature that we win souls for Jesus. We can become so mature that when we lay hands on the sick, they recover. We can become so mature that the gifts of the Holy Spirit will flow through our lives. God never told us to *go deep*—He simply said to *go out*.

The spirit of the world is always exalting self. "Gimmee, gimmee, gimmee, and get, get, get. No matter who I have to knock over, step on, or drag down, I am going to get my way. I am going to make it. I do not care who I hurt or destroy. I am going to become the big 'I', and I am going to be famous and well-known."

God, please help us! You can be in the religious world and have that attitude. You can be born again and have that attitude. You can be baptized in the Holy Spirit and have that attitude.

We need to have our "I" knocked out. Let us seek God until we have a spirit that honors others above ourselves. *Be kindly affectioned one to another with brotherly love; in honour preferring one another* (Romans 12:10).

The Bible says we have not received the spirit of the world. We have received the Spirit of God! *Now we have received, not the spirit of the world, but the spirit which is of God; that we might know the things that are freely given to us of God* (1 Corinthians 2:12).

Paul states four important truths in this passage of Scripture:

1 We have not received the spirit of the world.
2 We have received the Spirit that is of God.
3 We have received the Holy Spirit that we might know some things.
4 God has freely given us blessings.

Many beautiful Christians deny the work of the Holy Spirit. Generally, this is followed by a lack of faith for healing, deliverance from demonic forces, using the wonderful Name of Jesus, and receiving blessings freely given to us of God.

Yes, thanks be to God because He has given us His Spirit that we might KNOW. His Spirit will take us beyond believing into KNOWING.

I was a born-again Christian and Baptist minister for nineteen years, but it was only when the Lord Jesus baptized me in the Holy Ghost that I really began to understand what I had been freely given by God. There is a continual unfolding of the Lord Jesus Christ, and I have not arrived!

Paul, approximately four years before his death, exhibited in his letter to the Philippians a perfect spirit and example for us to follow.

> *But what things were gain to me, those I counted loss for Christ. Yea doubtless, and I count all things but loss for the excellency of the knowledge of Christ Jesus my Lord: for whom I have suffered the loss of all things, and do count them but dung, that I may win Christ, and be found in him, not having mine own righteousness, which is of the law, but that which is through the faith of Christ, the righteousness which is of God by faith: that I may know him, and the power of his resurrection, and the fellowship of his sufferings, being made conformable unto his death* (Philippians 3:7-10).

My prayer is that I might KNOW Him and the power of His resurrection. I have not yet begun to know Jesus as I want to know Him. I WANT TO KNOW JESUS—*In whom are hid all the treasures of wisdom and knowledge* (Colossians 2:3).

These treasures, these blessings, are hidden in Him. I WANT YOU TO KNOW THAT YOU HAVE MANY BLESSINGS IN CHRIST JESUS!

In 2 Kings, the Bible tells a remarkable story. There were four lepers outside the city gates of Samaria. Within the city, the people were starving. They were so hungry that they were actually eating their own babies—they ate their own flesh and blood. There was no food and death was everywhere.

The Syrian army had camped outside the gates, and there were thousands of them.

> *And there were four leprous men at the entering in of the gate: and they said one to another, Why sit we here until we die?...And they rose up in the twilight, to go unto the camp of the Syrians: and when they were come to the uttermost part of the camp of Syria, behold, there was no man there. For the Lord had made the host of the Syrians to hear a noise of chariots, and a noise of horses, even the noise of a great host...Wherefore they arose and fled in the twilight, and left their tents...and fled for their life.*
>
> *And when these lepers came to the uttermost part of the camp, they went into one tent, and did eat and drink, and carried thence silver, and gold, and raiment...Then they said one to another, We do not well: this day is a day of good tidings, and we hold our peace: if we tarry till the morning light, some mischief will come upon us: now therefore come, that we may go and tell the king's household...And the people went out, and spoiled the tents of the Syrians. So a mea-*

*sure of fine flour was sold for a shekel, and two
measures of barley for a shekel, according to the
word of the Lord* (2 Kings 7:3,5-9,16).

Did you notice the first thing these lepers did?
They SAID to one another, "Why sit we here until
we die?"

The second thing they did was move. They
ROSE UP. When they acted, God did something
for them.

Third, the lepers MOVED toward the enemy.
God caused the host of the Syrian army to hear a
noise of chariots. That great army fled in terror,
leaving all their supplies.

Now I want you to say what God's Word says.
Why sit ye there and die? Rise up! Go toward those
encamped against you, and the devil will flee from
you in terror!

While the lepers were in the tents eating plen-
ty of food, many in the city were starving. Why
were the lepers eating? Because they said something, rose up, *and moved toward the enemy!*

In the city of Samaria, people were starving.
They had no hope. Food was available, but they
did not have KNOWLEDGE of it. Some of us have
left the camp and gone after the enemy. We have
been to the household of the King, and we can tell
you, THE FAMINE IS OVER!

Yes, there is a universal call on humanity
through Jesus Christ! *Ho, every one that thirsteth,
come ye to the waters, and he that hath no money; come*

ye, buy, and eat; yea, come, buy wine and milk without money and without price (Isaiah 55:1).

Thank God, He is pouring out His Spirit upon all flesh. Living water is available to all without measure.

You may be facing a death sentence from some dreadful disease. You may be facing a great disappointment. This book is written for you!

Rise up in your spirit. Use God's Word as a weapon. God's Spirit will enforce His Word, and it will be *according to the Word of the Lord.*

Do you know what I see? I see God's people remaining behind denominational walls, walls of tradition, and walls of ignorance to the Word of God. They do not know what He has already freely given to them.

I am one of those tongue-talking, despised lepers coming to tell you, "The famine is over. Yea, come, buy wine and milk without money and without price." Jesus paid the price—and it was not cheap. The price He paid includes anything that we will ever need as long as we are on the earth. The price He paid includes eternal life with Him.

You may already be a member of the household of the King, or you may have never heard the message of salvation. It does not matter to God. He loves you either way. God wants you to partake of the blessings that He has freely given you.

Perhaps you have sat in the city and never enjoyed your blessings. You may be starving to death, but the blessings are yours! If you have received Jesus Christ, you are of the household of the King! Let's look at seven things that are yours in Christ.

I. WE ARE SAVED

The first thing we have in Christ is salvation. I want you to boldly say, "I AM SAVED."

You may say, "I know I am saved." Well, it is good to know it again. Many people know they are saved today, but tomorrow when they stub their toe and say something ugly, they think, "Well, I would not dare say I am saved now."

There is an assurance and a stability that every child of God can have. They can say without a doubt, "I know I am saved."

Do not insult God's Word by coming down the aisle every time an invitation is given for salvation.

> *But what saith it? The word is nigh thee, even in thy mouth, and in thy heart: that is, the word of faith, which we preach; that if thou shalt confess with thy mouth the Lord Jesus, and shalt believe in thine heart that God hath raised him from the dead, thou shalt be saved. For with the heart man believeth unto righteousness; and with the mouth confession is made unto salvation. For the scripture saith, Whosoever believeth on him shall not be ashamed* (Romans 10:8-11).

Now YOU say: "I confess with my mouth, that Jesus is my Lord. I believe in my heart that God raised Him from the dead. Therefore, I am saved. I AM SAVED!"

Now, did God promise that? Yes. GOD SAID IT!

You are not saying something that you made up. You are not saying something based on your own feelings. You are saying what God himself has said.

When you believe in your heart that God raised Jesus from the dead and confess that He is your Lord, you have a Bible right to say, I AM SAVED! *But as many as received him, to them gave he power to become the sons of God, even to them that believe on his name* (John 1:12).

Have you received Jesus as your Lord? If you confess that you have received Him, this passage of Scripture is speaking about YOU. God gave you the power (the authority and right) to become sons of God. You are a child of God.

If anyone ever questions your right to say that you are a child of God, remember that according to Romans 10:9-10, you can boldly declare: "I confess with my mouth that Jesus is my Lord. I believe in my heart that God raised Him from the dead. Therefore, I am saved." And according to John 1:12, "Because I have received Jesus, I am a child of God."

Therefore, you can boldly say that God has given you the authority and the right to be known as a son or a daughter of God. *For God so loved the world, that he gave his only begotten Son, that whosoever believeth in him should not perish, but have everlasting life. For God sent not his Son into the world to condemn the world; but that the world through him might be saved* (John 3:16-17).

God wants us to know that we are saved. He wants us to know that we are His children. *Verily, verily, I say unto you, He that heareth my word, and believeth on him that sent me, hath everlasting life, and shall not come into condemnation; but is passed from death unto life* (John 5:24).

Some of you are waiting to die to see if you are going to pass the test. I want to tell you, "YOU HAVE ALREADY PASSED IT!" You have already passed out of death into life! You have confessed with your mouth that Jesus is Lord. You have believed in your heart that God raised Him from the dead. God has given you power to become His child. You have passed from death unto life. YOU HAVE ETERNAL LIFE!

Thank God! I want you to say, "I know I am saved. I have received Jesus as my Lord and Saviour. I boldly confess that I am saved."

IN CHRIST, we have the right to KNOW that we are saved, and the right to KNOW that we have eternal life.

II. WE ARE BORN AGAIN

The second thing we have in Christ is the born-again experience. I want you to say, "I AM BORN AGAIN."

In the third chapter of John, Jesus was speaking to one of the most religious men of His day, Nicodemus, a devout Pharisee. He came to Jesus by night because religion did not and would never satisfy him.

You can be involved in all kinds of religions and still die and go to hell because you are not born again! You must be born again! Your spirit must have a new birth.

> *Jesus answered and said unto him, Verily, verily, I say unto thee, Except a man be born again, he cannot see the kingdom of God. Nicodemus saith unto him, How can a man be born when he is old? can he enter the second time into his mother's womb, and be born? Jesus answered, Verily, verily, I say unto thee, Except a man be born of water and of the Spirit, he cannot enter into the kingdom of God. That which is born of the flesh is flesh; and that which is born of the Spirit is spirit* (John 3:3-6).

Thank God, when we receive Jesus, WE ARE BORN AGAIN. *But as many as received him, to them gave he power to become the sons of God, even to them that believe on his name: which were born, not of blood, nor of the will of the flesh, nor of the will of man, but of God* (John 1:12-13).

You are born of God! When you receive Jesus Christ as your Lord, you experience the new birth in your spirit. *Being born again, not of corruptible seed, but of incorruptible, by the word of God, which liveth and abideth for ever* (1 Peter 1:23).

The new birth is like a natural birth in that you know there can be no birth without the implantation of a seed. Through the seed in a woman's body, our bodies were brought forth. The new birth takes place when a seed is planted in your spirit. That seed is the Word of God.

Nothing productive can take place in our lives until we have planted His Word inside us. The seed of God's Word in us is incorruptible, imperishable—it lives forever!

God's Word is the seed for every area of our lives, but we must take time to plant it inside of our spirit.

One day someone came along and planted a seed inside of you and me. They gave us the Gospel.

> *Moreover, brethren, I declare unto you the gospel which I preached unto you, which also ye have received, and wherein ye stand; by which also ye are saved, if ye keep in memory what I preached unto you, unless ye have believed in vain. For I delivered unto you first of all that which I also received, how that Christ died for our sins according to the scriptures; and that he was buried, and that he rose again the third day according to the scriptures* (1 Corinthians 15:1-4).

The Gospel consists of three facts:
1 Christ died for our sins.
2 He was buried.

3 He rose again.

Someone declared to us the Gospel. We believed it and united our faith with God's Word, that incorruptible seed, and inside of us a birth took place.

After I received Jesus, I looked just as I always did on the outside, but inside I was a new creature. You see, I was born again! I had a new kind of LIFE inside, and I knew that I was born again. I had no desire to be with those who were unsaved. A change had taken place in me.

Make this confession: "I AM SAVED. I AM BORN AGAIN." Repeat it boldly: "I AM SAVED. I AM BORN AGAIN."

Now, do not cast away your confidence. You may stumble and go back into the old life momentarily, but hold fast to your testimony. Say aloud, "I am miserable in this sin. Father, forgive me. Thank You, Lord, for cleansing me. Thank God, I know I am saved! I know I am born again." *If we confess our sins, he is faithful and just to forgive us our sins, and to cleanse us from all unrighteousness* (1 John 1:9).

When God saves us, He puts a light on the inside of us. *Ye are the light of the world. A city that is set on an hill cannot be hid* (Matthew 5:14).

I want you to say, "I AM THE LIGHT OF THE WORLD!"

That is exactly what God says about you and me. He put a light on the inside of us. Do you have Jesus on the inside of you? He is the Light of the world.

Some people have the idea that they are like a blinker light. They think they go on and off. Jesus does not go on and off in me. He keeps on shining.

Many people wear themselves out. They think they are running from kingdom to kingdom. One moment they think they are in the kingdom of light; the next moment they think they are in the kingdom of darkness.

We need to make a firm decision to believe God's Word. When we receive Jesus as our Lord and Savior, His light in us does not go out. We are indeed in the KINGDOM OF LIGHT. The Light of lights dwells in us, and our light will never go out!

> *Before anything else existed, there was Christ, with God. He has always been alive and is himself God. He created everything there is— nothing exists that he didn't make. Eternal life is in him, and this life gives light to all mankind. His life is the light that shines through the darkness—and the darkness can never extinguish it* (John 1:1-5, TLB).

III. WE ARE MADE NEW CREATURES

The third thing we have in Christ is a newly created spirit. I want you to say, "I AM A NEW CREATURE IN CHRIST JESUS."

The Bible says we are saved, we are born again, and we are made new creatures. Inside your body,

41

when you accepted Jesus, there burst into being a new creation. *Therefore if any man be in Christ, he is a new creature: old things are passed away; behold, all things become new* (2 Corinthians 5:17).

Did you know that when you became a new creation, not only was your past forgiven, but your past also ceased to exist?

Have you ever held a newborn baby in your arms and thought, "How wonderful—a new beginning!"? A newborn baby does not have a past.

The new creation in you has no past! Whether it is divorce, murder, homosexuality, lesbianism, or any other form of sin, YOUR PAST DOES NOT EXIST!

You are a newborn baby. You are a new creature. Old things are passed away and, behold, all things are become new. YOU ARE A NEW CREATION!

This new creation has the life of God—everlasting life. The moment you make the decision to believe on the Lord Jesus Christ, you are no longer condemned. *For God sent not his Son into the world to condemn the world; but that the world through him might be saved. He that believeth on him is not condemned: but he that believeth not is condemned already, because he hath not believed in the name of the only begotten Son of God* (John 3:17:18).

God assures us, "I will not remember thy sins." Sins are wrong acts that are committed against an established law, even if the law is not known. *I, even*

I, am he that blotteth out thy transgressions for mine own sake, and will not remember thy sins (Isaiah 43:25).

God further assures us, "I have blotted out thy transgressions." Transgressions are wrong acts committed in open disobedience of a known law. *I have blotted out, as a thick cloud, thy transgressions, and, as a cloud, thy sins…*(Isaiah 44:22a).

The Prophet Isaiah compared sins and transgressions. Sins are as a cloud. Transgressions are as a thick cloud.

From Isaiah's comparison, we understand that transgressions are the darker of the two. Thank God, He not only cleared us of the past, but He made provision for us if we commit transgressions after we have come to know Christ as Savior. *If we confess our sins, he is faithful and just to forgive us our sins, and to cleanse us from all unrighteousness* (1 John 1:9).

If a believer sins and thereafter repents and confesses his sins, both he and the record of his life are completely cleansed.

If you are grieved when you sin, do not be sad. You should be happy because that is a sign that you are a new creature in Christ Jesus.

> *No one born (begotten) of God [deliberately, knowingly, and habitually] practices sin, for God's nature abides in him [His principle of life, the divine sperm, remains permanently within him]; and he cannot practice sinning because he is born (begotten) of God* (1 John 3:9, Amplified).

Make this confession:

"I am a new creature in Christ Jesus. I am no longer condemned. God does not remember my sins. All my sins have been blotted out. I am a new creature—I have no past. If I sin, I will immediately confess my sins. I will immediately be cleansed from all unrighteousness. Thank God, I am a new creature! Thank God, I have eternal life! Thank God, I will never die!"

IV. WE ARE DELIVERED

The fourth thing we have in Christ is deliverance. I want you to say, I AM DELIVERED!

> *Giving thanks unto the Father, which hath made us meet to be partakers of the inheritance of the saints in light: who hath delivered us from the power of darkness, and hath translated us into the kingdom of his dear Son* (Colossians 1:12-13).

WE ARE SAVED. WE ARE BORN AGAIN. WE ARE NEW CREATURES. WE ARE DELIVERED.

What have we been delivered from? We have been delivered from the power and the authority of darkness. Some of you may be fighting old habits. You may be struggling against old ways. Perhaps you do not know that you have the power IN YOU to overcome these obstacles. I want to tell you that *you have already been delivered!*

You must get mad at the devil and say, "Devil, I command you in the Name of Jesus to take your hands off me! I AM DELIVERED!"

I am he that liveth, and was dead; and, behold, I am alive for evermore, Amen; and have the keys of hell and of death (Revelation 1:18).

Boldly tell the devil, "Jesus holds the keys to hell and to death, and no devil can take my life. No demon can harm me or steal one day of my life."

God is still God, and He has already delivered you! You do not have to put up with those whirling thoughts of depression that come over you at times. You do not have to put up with those mental battles. RISE UP! Get mad at the devil and boldly declare your deliverance.

You are not *going* to be delivered. You *are* delivered! You now walk in the kingdom of light. You have been translated into the kingdom of Jesus. *For ye were sometimes darkness, but now are ye light in the Lord: walk as children of light* (Ephesians 5:8).

Act like you are in the light. Declare your deliverance because you have it. Make this confession: "I am delivered from the power of darkness. I am in the kingdom of light."

V. WE ARE REDEEMED

The fifth thing we have in Christ is redemption. I want you to say, "I AM REDEEMED."

> *Christ hath redeemed us from the curse of the law, being made a curse for us: for it is written, Cursed is every one that hangeth on a tree: that the blessing of Abraham might come on the Gentiles through Jesus Christ; that we might receive the promise of the Spirit through faith* (Galatians 3:13-14).

God states clearly that this redemption is based upon our response to His requirement: *But it shall come to pass, if thou wilt not hearken unto the voice of the Lord thy God, to observe to do all his commandments and his statutes which I command thee this day; that all these curses shall come upon thee, and overtake thee* (Deuteronomy 28:15).

God, through Jesus Christ, has given every man a choice. *I call heaven and earth to record this day against you, that I have set before you life and death, blessing and cursing: therefore choose life, that both thou and thy seed may live: that thou mayest love the Lord thy God, and that thou mayest obey his voice, and that thou mayest cleave unto him: for he is thy life, and the length of thy days...* (Deuteronomy 30:19-20a).

When we accept Jesus Christ as our Savior, we choose life, and we are redeemed. What are we redeemed from? We are redeemed from the curse of the law!

I want you to say: "I choose life. I am redeemed from the curse of the law."

The Bible clearly defines the curse of the law in the twenty-eighth chapter of Deuteronomy:

Cursed in the city	Plagues
Cursed in the field	Emerods
Cursed in the basket	Scabs
Cursed in the store	Itch
Children are cursed	Madness
Land is cursed	Blindness
Livestock is cursed	Fever
Cursed when coming in	Poverty
Cursed when going out	Darkness
Vexation	Oppression
Rebuke	Adultery
Complete Destruction	Powerless
Pestilence	Despair
Will serve enemies	Boils
Astonishment of heart	Captivity
Extreme burning	Idolatry
You will be dispersed	Drought
Enemies will smite thee	Mildew
Heaven will be brass	Sword (war)
Earth will be iron	Unburied
Disappointment	Consumption
Children will go away	Children will return

These are the grave consequences of disobedience. This is the misery of sin. But, thank God, we are redeemed from the curse of the law! *O give thanks unto the Lord, for he is good: for his mercy endureth for ever. Let the redeemed of the Lord say so, whom he hath redeemed from the hand of the enemy* (Psalm 107:1-2).

David said, "Let the redeemed of the Lord SAY so." Say, "I AM REDEEMED."

Look in the mirror and say these things. Say them to your wife or husband. "I AM SAVED. I AM BORN AGAIN. I AM A NEW CREATURE. I AM DELIVERED. I AM REDEEMED."

Say it so the devil can hear you. Say it so every demon can hear you. Say it so the angels will rejoice with you!

> *Forasmuch as ye know that ye were not redeemed with corruptible things, as silver and gold, from your vain conversation received by tradition from your fathers; but with the precious blood of Christ, as of a lamb without blemish and without spot* (1 Peter 1:18-19).

The price of our redemption is the precious blood of Jesus.

> *But Christ being come an high priest of good things to come, by a greater and more perfect tabernacle, not made with hands, that is to say, not of this building; neither by the blood of goats and calves, but by his own blood he entered in once into the holy place, having obtained eternal redemption for us* (Hebrews 9:11-12).

Jesus obtained eternal redemption for us with His own blood! You see, Christ gathered up His blood. Not a drop was left on the earth. He ascended to heaven, and there, in the presence of the Father, He presented His blood.

> *For ye are not come unto the mount that might be touched, and that burned with fire, nor*

unto blackness, and darkness, and tempest, and the sound of a trumpet, and the voice of words; which voice they that heard entreated that the word should not be spoken to them any more: (For they could not endure that which was commanded, And if so much as a beast touch the mountain, it shall be stoned, or thrust through with a dart: And so terrible was the sight, that Moses said, I exceedingly fear and quake:) but ye are come unto mount Sion, and unto the city of the living God, the heavenly Jerusalem, and to an innumerable company of angels, to the general assembly and church of the firstborn, which are written in heaven, and to God the Judge of all, and to the spirits of just men made perfect, and to Jesus the mediator of the new covenant, and to the blood of sprinkling, that speaketh better things than that of Abel (Hebrews 12:18-24).*

The blood of Jesus Christ is ever before the Father as evidence that we have been redeemed from every oppressive curse and every wicked work of the devil. *In whom we have redemption through his blood, the forgiveness of sins, according to the riches of his grace* (Ephesians 1:7). Through the blood of Jesus, WE ARE REDEEMED!

In the Old Testament, God instructed the children of Israel to kill a lamb, and to put the blood on their door posts. This is known as the Passover, and it protected them from the death angel. *And the blood shall be to you for a token upon the houses where ye are: and when I see the blood, I will pass over you, and the plague shall not be upon you to destroy you, when I smite the land of Egypt* (Exodus 12:13).

In the New Testament, Jesus celebrated the Passover with His disciples. He took the cup and spoke these words: *For this is my blood of the new testament, which is shed for many for the remission of sins. But I say unto you, I will not drink henceforth of this fruit of the vine, until that day when I drink it new with you in my Father's kingdom* (Matthew 26:28-29).

Jesus himself was offered for the sins of the world. His blood was shed for our sins—He paid the price. But the responsibility of applying the blood of Jesus to the door posts of our lives rests upon us. *Seeing then that we have a great high priest, that is passed into the heavens, Jesus the Son of God, let us hold fast our profession* [confession] (Hebrews 4:14).

By our confession, we testify to Satan and all the demonic forces what the Word of God says the blood of Jesus does for us! *And they overcame him* [Satan] *by the blood of the Lamb, and by the word of their testimony* [confession]; *and they loved not their lives unto the death* (Revelation 12:11).

God is looking for blood on the door posts of our lives. Where He does not find the blood of Jesus there is no protection. He is not interested in which church we attend—he simply requires that we accept His Son as Savior.

When the devil tries to give you an evil desire or a wicked imagination, remind him of the blood that bought your redemption. Say boldly: "Through the blood of Jesus, I am redeemed! I am redeemed from the curse of the law!"

VI. WE ARE BLESSED

The sixth thing we have in Christ is the blessing of Abraham. I want you to say, "I AM BLESSED."

> *Christ hath redeemed us from the curse of the law, being made a curse for us: for it is written, Cursed is every one that hangeth on a tree: that the blessing of Abraham might come on the Gentiles through Jesus Christ; that we might receive the promise of the Spirit through faith* (Galatians 3:13-14).

I want you to say: "I AM SAVED. I AM BORN AGAIN. I AM A NEW CREATURE. I AM DELIVERED. I AM REDEEMED. I AM BLESSED."

> *And it shall come to pass, if thou shalt hearken diligently unto the voice of the Lord thy God, to observe and to do all his commandments which I command thee this day, that the Lord thy God will set thee on high above all nations of the earth: and all these blessings shall come on thee, and overtake thee, if thou shalt hearken unto the voice of the Lord thy God* (Deuteronomy 28:1-2).

In the twenty-eighth chapter of Deuteronomy, we find the blessing of Abraham:

Blessed in the city
Blessed in the field
Children will be blessed
Land will be blessed
Livestock will be blessed
Basket will be blessed
Blessed coming in
Blessed going out
Enemies will flee from you seven ways
Blessed in storehouses
Blessed in all you put your hand to
Established as a holy people
People can see that you are called by the Name
of the Lord (that you live in the presence
of the Lord)
People of the earth will be afraid of you
Surplus of prosperity through the fruit of your
body, livestock, and ground
The Lord will give rain to your land
The Lord will bless all the work of your hand
You will lend and not borrow
You will be the head and not the tail
You will be above only and not beneath.

If you study Abraham's life, you will find that he was never sick. His wife was so beautiful at ninety years of age that another man wanted her. The Bible says, *Abraham was very rich in cattle, silver and gold* (Genesis 13:2).

If you are in a financial crisis, read the first fourteen verses of Deuteronomy, chapter twenty-eight, and remember that CHRIST HAS REDEEM-

ED YOU FROM THE CURSE OF THE LAW IN ORDER THAT THE BLESSING OF ABRAHAM MIGHT COME ON YOU THROUGH JESUS CHRIST.

Let your eyes rest on the blessing of Abraham, as you meditate day and night on these promises of God:

- Your financial situation will turn around.
- Your land will be blessed.
- Your children will be blessed.
- Your cattle will be blessed.
- Your enemies will flee from you.
- You will be known as a holy people.
- Your business will be blessed.

Begin to partake of these great blessings that God has provided for you and your family.

VII. WE ARE OVERCOMERS

The seventh thing we have in Christ is the ability to be an overcomer. I want you to say, "I HAVE OVERCOME."

Ye are of God, little children, and have overcome them: because greater is he that is in you, than he that is in the world (1 John 4:4).

What does it mean to overcome? It means *to win the victory over.* You may say, "Now, Brother Osteen, just a minute. There is no way I can have victory in my situation."

Yes, you can! Let your eyes go back to that verse and begin to meditate on what God said through the Apostle John. Because God is in you, you *have* overcome.

Have you paused long enough today to remember that you are not in the battle alone? God is on the inside of you. Yes, God dwells in you. *Know ye not that ye are the temple of God, and that the Spirit of God dwelleth in you?* (1 Corinthians 3:16).

We are of God—we are not of this world. We are *in* the world, but we are not *of* the world. We do not belong to this world.

Do not remain a child in your Christian life. Begin to understand how you have been blessed. *Now I say, That the heir, as long as he is a child, differeth nothing from a servant, though he be lord of all* (Galatians 4:1).

God, through Jesus Christ, has brought total victory in every area of our lives, but we must enforce that victory. When you open your heart and receive these great truths, you can be lord of all. You can overcome sickness, depression, fear, torment, and every other curse of the law.

God predestined us to be VICTORIOUS over:

Evil influences of men—*Through thee will we push down our enemies: through thy name will we tread them under that rise up against us* (Psalm 44:5).

Demonic forces—*Behold, I give unto you power to tread on serpents and scorpions, and over all the power of the enemy: and nothing shall by any means hurt you* (Luke 10:19).

Circumstances of life—*Who shall separate us from the love of Christ? Shall tribulation, or distress, or persecution, or famine, or nakedness, or peril, or sword? Nay, in all these things we are more than conquerors through him that loved us* (Romans 8:35,37).

Now thanks be unto God, which always causeth us to triumph in Christ, and maketh manifest the savour of his knowledge by us in every place (2 Corinthians 2:14).

Worldly attractions—*For whatsoever is born of God overcometh the world: and this is the victory that overcometh the world, even our faith* (1 John 5:4).

Satanic power at the end of the age—*And I saw as it were a sea of glass mingled with fire: and them that had gotten the victory over the beast, and over his image, and over his mark, and over the number of his name, stand on the sea of glass, having the harps of God* (Revelation 15:2).

You may be in a battle today for your life, but YOU CAN OVERCOME! Take the Word of God and the blood of Jesus, and defeat the devil. You can do it because greater is He that is in you than he that is in the world! *And they overcame him* [Satan] *by the blood of the Lamb, and by the word of their testimony; and they loved not their lives unto the death* (Revelation 12:11).

Let us imagine that we are at the throne of God. Jesus—His beloved Son who bears the marks of Calvary—is at His right hand. He loves us with an everlasting love. He is the visible representation of the invisible God. He is God manifested in the flesh, and He is sitting at the right hand of the Father.

Angels are lingering near. Satan, the accuser of the brethren, has come to accuse us. There is God, our Father and Jesus, the High Priest of our confession.

In the presence of Jesus, we want to tell the Father something. We want to say, "WE ARE SAVED. WE ARE BORN AGAIN. WE ARE NEW CREATURES. WE ARE DELIVERED. WE ARE REDEEMED. WE ARE BLESSED. WE ARE OVERCOMERS."

Now I want you to say it just for yourself. "I AM SAVED. I AM BORN AGAIN. I AM A NEW CREATURE. I AM DELIVERED. I AM REDEEMED. I AM BLESSED. I HAVE OVERCOME!"

The Father smiles, Jesus rejoices, angels dance for you, and the devil trembles!

4

A Confession of Deliverance from Satan's Power

Today, many people are oppressed by Satan. They are miserable and tormented, and as a result, they talk of demons and their work constantly. Actually, without realizing what they are doing, they are boasting of Satan.

If you are doing that—stop such foolishness! Let your eyes rest on the scriptures listed on the following pages. Let your mind dwell on the eternal truths set forth in these verses. Meditate on them. They helped me, and they will help you.

Boldly take the Word of God and make it your confession. Read these scriptures aloud. Deliberately come before the throne of God with His Word and with this confession, and watch Satan flee from you!

Train yourself to confess these truths constantly. Remember, what you continue to say with your mouth and believe in your heart will come to pass in your life. Never allow your mouth to speak what is contrary to God's Word.

> *Let us therefore come boldly unto the throne of grace, that we may obtain mercy, and find grace to help in time of need* (Hebrews 4:16).

> *Wherefore, holy brethren, partakers of the heavenly calling, consider the Apostle and High Priest of our profession, Christ Jesus* (Hebrews 3:1).

> *Take with you words, and turn to the Lord: say unto him, Take away all iniquity, and receive us graciously: so will we render the calves of our lips* (Hosea 14:2).

> *And this is the confidence that we have in him, that, if we ask any thing according to his will, he heareth us: and if we know that he hear us, whatsoever we ask, we know that we have the petitions that we desired of him* (1 John 5:14-15).

> *Death and life are in the power of the tongue: and they that love it shall eat the fruit thereof* (Proverbs 18:21).

> *For verily I say unto you, That whosoever shall say unto this mountain, Be thou removed, and be thou cast into the sea; and shall not doubt in his heart, but shall believe that those things which he saith shall come to pass; he shall have whatsoever he saith* (Mark 11:23).

Who hath delivered us from the power of darkness, and hath translated us into the kingdom of his dear Son (Colossians 1:13).

And you hath he quickened, who were dead in trespasses and sins; wherein in time past ye walked according to the course of this world, according to the prince of the power of the air, the spirit that now worketh in the children of disobedience (Ephesians 2:1-2).

Neither give place to the devil (Ephesians 4:27).

For the kingdom of God is not meat and drink; but righteousness, and peace, and joy in the Holy Ghost (Romans 14:17).

But seek ye first the kingdom of God, and his righteousness; and all these things shall be added unto you (Matthew 6:33).

Behold, I give unto you power to tread on serpents and scorpions, and over all the power of the enemy: and nothing shall by any means hurt you (Luke 10:19).

And these signs shall follow them that believe; In my name shall they cast out devils; they shall speak with new tongues (Mark 16:17).

Submit yourselves therefore to God. Resist the devil, and he will flee from you (James 4:7).

And they overcame him by the blood of the Lamb, and by the word of their testimony; and they loved not their lives unto the death (Revelation 12:11).

He that committeth sin is of the devil; for the devil sinneth from the beginning. For this purpose the Son of God was manifested, that he might destroy the works of the devil (1 John 3:8).

And having spoiled principalities and powers, he made a show of them openly, triumphing over them in it (Colossians 2:15).

Or else how can one enter into a strong man's house, and spoil his goods, except he first bind the strong man? and then he will spoil his house (Matthew 12:29).

Nay, in all these things we are more than conquerors through him that loved us (Romans 8:37).

This is the day which the Lord hath made; we will rejoice and be glad in it (Psalm 118:24).

A CONFESSION OF DELIVERANCE FROM SATAN'S POWER

"Father, as I approach Your throne now with my confession, I know the Word of God says, *Let us therefore come boldly unto the throne of grace, that we may obtain mercy, and find grace to help in time of need* (Hebrews 4:16). As I come to boldly confess, I realize that Jesus is the High Priest of my confession (see Hebrews 3:1). You said, *Take with you words, and turn to the Lord...*(Hosea 14:2).

"Father, I come to Your throne today in the face of all the doubt...in the face of all the assaults of the devil...in the face of all the forces of darkness...TO BOLDLY CONFESS YOUR WORD!

"Lord, I know that You listen to me when I pray and speak to You according to Your Word. The Word of God says that if we ask anything according to Your will (Your Word), you hear us. And if You hear us, we know we have the petitions we ask of You (see 1 John 5:14-15).

"Father, I know that my confession is important because *Death and life are in the power of the tongue...* (Proverbs 18:21).

"Lord, You said in Your Word that I could have whatever I say (see Mark 11:23). I boldly confess Your Word today concerning myself as a new creature in Christ Jesus. I come with that Word in my mouth, believing it in my heart.

"I boldly declare before You, Father, before the Lord Jesus Christ, and before the demonic forces of hell:

I AM BORN AGAIN! I AM REDEEMED! I AM DELIVERED!

"Father, I want to dwell upon Your Word that You have spoken to me. Your Word says that I am delivered from the power of darkness and translated into the kingdom of Your dear Son (see Colossians 1:13).

"Father, I thank You that I am not *going* to be delivered, but I AM DELIVERED!

"I know that Your Word teaches me that there are two kingdoms—a kingdom of light and a kingdom of darkness. I know that in the kingdom of darkness there is misery, demonic power, doubt, unforgiveness of sins, sickness, oppression, deep depression, and mental anguish.

"I know that in the kingdom of darkness, Satan is lord. There are demonic forces which harass and vex the members of that kingdom. I once walked in that kingdom when I was lost. As Your Word says, …[I] *walked according to the course of this world, according to…the spirit that now worketh in the children of disobedience* (Ephesians 2:2). That evil spirit did work in me. I walked in that darkness and was so unhappy. I did not have the joy of the Lord. I did not have eternal life. I walked according to the course of this world.

"But, Father, I thank You that one day the Lord Jesus became my Lord and my Savior. I thank You that one day You called me into fellowship with Him. By Your grace and mercy, You revealed Jesus to me, and I made Him my Lord. When I made Jesus my Lord, I was delivered from the powers of darkness and translated into the kingdom of Your dear Son!

"Father, I want to remind you that I HAVE BEEN DELIVERED! I want to remind the Lord Jesus Christ, and the holy angels of God!

"Satan, I remind you and all the demon forces that follow you that I HAVE BEEN DELIVERED! I am delivered by the power of Jesus Christ, by His Name and by His blood! I am delivered from the power of darkness, and I have been translated into the KINGDOM OF LIGHT!

"You have no authority over me, Satan. You have no power over me, Satan. It is only my ignorance that has given you any power over me. The Bible says, *Neither give place to the devil* (Ephesians 4:27).

"Satan, I have given you a place in my life at times, but I will not do it anymore. You have no authority and no power over me whatsoever! I have been delivered from all of your power. Satan, I command you, IN THE NAME OF THE LORD JESUS CHRIST, to leave me now!

"Father, I rejoice that the devil has no legal or spiritual authority over me whatsoever. I am walking and living in the kingdom of light—the kingdom of Your Son. *For the kingdom of God is...righteousness, and peace, and joy in the Holy Ghost* (Romans 14:17).

"Lord, Your kingdom is not sickness, depression, evil and wickedness, oppression, vexation, trouble, and sorrow.

"I walk in the kingdom of God, which is righteousness, peace, and joy in the Holy Ghost.

"Oh hallelujah! I praise You, Lord! I am in the kingdom of righteousness, the kingdom of peace, and the kingdom of joy in the Holy Ghost!

"Jesus, You said, *But seek ye first the kingdom of God, and his righteousness; and all these things shall be added unto you* (Matthew 6:33). Father, I seek first the kingdom of God. I am putting Your kingdom first this day. I know that as I am obedient to Your Word, all the problems and all the things I have before me will be taken care of. That is Your business. My business is to seek FIRST the kingdom of God.

"As I seek first the kingdom of God, my family will be taken care of...my business will prosper ...and my prayers will be answered.

"I rejoice today that I am delivered from the power of darkness. Lord, You said in Your Word, *Behold, I give unto you power to tread on serpents and scorpions, and over all the power of the enemy: and nothing shall by any means hurt you* (Luke 10:19). You were talking to me, Lord, and to all believers.

"Oh, Father, I confess boldly with my mouth: I have power to tread on serpents and scorpions, which are demon powers. I have power over all the power of the enemy, and nothing shall by any means hurt me.

"It is almost too big for me to understand, and yet I accept in my spirit that I have power in the Name of the Lord Jesus Christ and by the power of His blood—not over one demon, one hundred demons, or one thousand demons, but over every demonic force, all the demon forces combined, and over the devil himself!

"You have given me power over all the power of the enemy and nothing shall by any means hurt me—not what I have done in the past (which has ceased to exist), not what I face now, or what I shall face in the future. NOTHING SHALL BY ANY MEANS HURT ME!

"I know that the Word of God says, *...In my name shall they cast out devils...* (Mark 16:17). The Bible also says, *...Resist the devil, and he will flee from you* (James 4:7).

"In the light of God's Word, I come against every demonic force that is arrayed against me, my family, my business, and everything I am involved in. I COMMAND YOU, SATAN, TO LEAVE me, my family, all those for whom I am praying, and those in my circle of influence!

"I command you to take your hands off my business! I command you to take your hands off my children! I command you, IN THE NAME OF JESUS CHRIST, to take your hands off my spirit, mind, body, and all that I have to do today. Flee from me, Satan, according to the Word of God!

"Father, I praise You today because I am not subject to the devil. The devil is not my lord. JESUS IS MY LORD!

"In the Name of the Lord Jesus Christ, I have dispelled and caused to flee from me every demonic force! I am thankful that the Word of God says, *And they overcame him* [Satan] *by the blood of the Lamb, and by the word of their testimony; and they loved not their lives unto the death* (Revelation 12:11). By my confession of the Word of God, I hold up the blood of the Lord Jesus Christ.

"Satan, I boldly declare to you that the blood of Jesus is my shield and the Word of God is my testimony. Do not dare come near me or my household. You are a defeated foe. Your works have been destroyed. Jesus spoiled principalities and powers. He made a show of them openly, triumphing over them in the cross (see Colossians 2:15). Satan, you are spoiled and you are a defeated foe!

"Jesus said, *Or else how can one enter into a strong man's house, and spoil his goods, except he first bind the strong man? and then he will spoil his house* (Matthew 12:29). Jesus has already entered your house, Satan! He has taken from you all of your armor. He has spoiled your goods and divided His victory with me! He has shared His victory with every child of God!

"Therefore, Satan, I command you to leave me now! Take your thoughts and vexing powers and leave my mind, my children, my family, and my business. In the mighty Name of the Lord Jesus Christ, get behind me, Satan! I have power over you because I have been delivered from your authority. I have been translated into the kingdom of God's dear Son!

"Oh, Father, I thank You that I am in Your kingdom. I am not *going* to be, I *am*! I have been born into the kingdom of God, translated and transferred into the kingdom of light. Lord, I thank You that in this kingdom there is righteousness, peace, and joy in the Holy Ghost. I rejoice today because You are my Father, Jesus Christ is my Lord and Savior, and the Holy Ghost dwells within my body. I am more than a conqueror through Him that loves me. I am living in the kingdom of light, and I have no fear. I have been delivered from the power of darkness, and I have power over all the power of the enemy. I walk in righteousness, peace, and joy in the Holy Ghost. I rejoice and bless the Name of the Lord. This is the day the Lord has made. I choose to rejoice and be glad in it!

"I HAVE BEEN DELIVERED FROM SATAN'S POWER!"

5

A Confession of Strength to Overcome Every Attack of Satan

The Word of God is alive, and it is the sword of the Spirit. The Word of God, spoken out of our mouths, will defeat the devil!

Your enemy, Satan, is carefully organized. His purpose is to steal, kill, and destroy all that you hold dear. But do not be afraid of the devil!

God encourages us in His Word to be strong and very courageous. Read the Word of God, and speak the Word of God. It will penetrate the darkness around you. By speaking the Word of God, you will defeat the devil for yourself!

Finally, my brethren, be strong in the Lord, and in the power of his might. Put on the whole armour of God, that ye may be able to stand against the wiles of the devil. For we wrestle not against flesh and blood, but against principalities, against powers, against the rulers of the darkness of this world, against spiritual wickedness in high places. Wherefore take unto you the whole armour of God, that ye may be able to withstand in the evil day, and having done all, to stand. Stand therefore, having your loins girt about with truth, and having on the breastplate of righteousness; and your feet shod with the preparation of the gospel of peace; above all, taking the shield of faith, wherewith ye shall be able to quench all the fiery darts of the wicked. And take the helmet of salvation, and the sword of the Spirit, which is the word of God: praying always with all prayer and supplication in the Spirit, and watching thereunto with all perseverance and supplication for all saints... (Ephesians 6:10-18).

For verily I say unto you, That whosoever shall say unto this mountain, Be thou removed, and be thou cast into the sea; and shall not doubt in his heart, but shall believe that those things which he saith shall come to pass; he shall have whatsoever he saith (Mark 11:23).

Death and life are in the power of the tongue: and they that love it shall eat the fruit thereof (Proverbs 18:21).

Beat your plowshares into swords, and your pruninghooks into spears: let the weak say, I am strong (Joel 3:10).

I have written unto you, fathers, because ye have known him that is from the beginning. I have written unto you, young men, because ye are strong, and the word of God abideth in you, and ye have overcome the wicked one (1 John 2:14).

For this cause I bow my knees unto the Father of our Lord Jesus Christ, of whom the whole family in heaven and earth is named, that he would grant you, according to the riches of his glory, to be strengthened with might by his Spirit in the inner man (Ephesians 3:14-16).

The Lord is my light and my salvation; whom shall I fear? the Lord is the strength of my life; of whom shall I be afraid? (Psalm 27:1).

Therefore if any man be in Christ, he is a new creature: old things are passed away; behold, all things are become new (2 Corinthians 5:17).

The thief cometh not, but for to steal, and to kill, and to destroy: I am come that they might have life, and that they might have it more abundantly (John 10:10).

(For the weapons of our warfare are not carnal, but mighty through God to the pulling down of strong holds;) casting down imaginations, and every high thing that exalteth itself against the knowledge of God, and bringing into

71

captivity every thought to the obedience of Christ (2 Corinthians 10:4-5).

A CONFESSION OF STRENGTH TO OVERCOME EVERY ATTACK OF SATAN

"Father, I come today to make my confession of Your Word before Your great throne of mercy. I know that You are my Father. Lord Jesus, You are my Lord and Savior. The Holy Spirit dwells within my body, and I am covered with the blood of the Lord Jesus Christ. The angels of God attend my way.

"Lord, I do not believe all that my eyes see, all that my body feels, and all that the enemy would bring against me. I know that I shall rise no higher, nor sink lower than my confession.

"I dare to boldly confess Your Word! And as I confess Your Word, my body will line up with Your Word, my mind will obey Your Word, and my spirit will rise to the level of Your Word.

"I thank You that You have placed a law within us and within Your Word. We shall have whatsoever we say, and the power of life and death is in the tongue (see Mark 11:23 and Proverbs 18:21). Lord, I choose LIFE! Life is mine—not death.

"Father, I come to boldly declare that I am strong. I am strong spiritually, mentally, emotionally, physically, financially, and materially. I thank You that I am strong in my body, mind, and spirit. I AM STRONG!

"Lord, the Bible says, ...*let the weak say, I am strong* (Joel 3:10). It does not say, 'Let the weak pray.' It says, 'Let the weak SAY, I am strong.' Therefore I say I AM STRONG!

"Father, I boldly come to Your throne of grace and make my confession today according to Your Word. I am strong because the Word of God abides within me. I am strengthened with all might by Your Spirit in the inner man. I am strong because the Lord is my light and my salvation— whom shall I fear? The Lord is the strength of my life, of whom shall I be afraid? (see Psalm 27:1).

"The scriptures that I have before me today are true. I stand before Your throne and boldly confess out of my mouth, believing in my heart that these words are true. *Finally, my brethren, be strong in the Lord, and in the power of his might* (Ephesians 6:10).

"Lord, I declare that I am strong in You and in the power of Your might. First of all, Father, I want to thank You that I am in the Lord. I AM IN JESUS. ...*if any man be in Christ, he is a new creature...* (2 Corinthians 5:17). I am in Christ. I have redemption and all the blessings of God. I am in Jesus Christ, my Ark of Safety.

"I boldly say today, 'I am strong in the Lord and in the power of His might.' It does not matter what my body or my mind says, or what my circumstances may say. I am strong in the Lord and in the power of HIS might.

"Father, I put on Your whole armor, and I am able to stand against all the wiles and strategies of the devil. I know that Satan comes against me in every form and fashion, lying, stealing, and trying to destroy. But Jesus declared, *The thief cometh not, but for to steal, and to kill, and to destroy: I am come that they might have life, and that they might have it more abundantly* (John 10:10).

"Father, I know that anything that steals, kills, or destroys is of the devil; it is not of You. I thank You, Father, that I am able to stand against ALL the wiles of the devil. I know that I wrestle not against flesh and blood. Flesh and blood are not my enemies. I know that I wrestle against principalities, powers, the rulers of the darkness of this world, and wicked spirits in high places.

"Because of these wicked, evil spirits and demonic forces, I have taken unto me the whole armor of God. I am able to withstand in this evil day, and having done all and overcome all, I STAND! Father, there is NO fear in my heart or in my mind. I am an overcomer because I believe that Jesus Christ is the Son of God.

"I stand, therefore, having my loins girt about with truth. I have on the breastplate of righteousness. My feet are shod with the preparation of the gospel of peace. Above all, I have taken the shield of faith wherewith I quench all the fiery darts of the wicked. I have on the helmet of salvation, and I take the sword of the Spirit, which is the Word of God. I am praying always with all prayer and supplication in the Spirit and watching thereunto with all perseverance for all saints.

"Father, I thank You today that I am not a baby Christian. I am a mature Christian, dressed for battle. I am a soldier of the Lord Jesus Christ. The Bible says, *Thou therefore endure hardness, as a good soldier of Jesus Christ* (2 Timothy 2:3).

"I take the Word of God, and I boldly declare that I have on God's armor and I am strong. I have all power over all the power of the enemy, and nothing shall by any means hurt me!

"Lord, I thank You that the weapons of my warfare are not carnal, but mighty through God to the pulling down of strongholds, casting down imaginations, and bringing every thought into the captivity of Christ (see 2 Corinthians 10:4-5).

"I have the blood of Jesus Christ and the Name of Jesus Christ today. I have the nature of God and the Holy Spirit in my body today.

"I rejoice and bless the Name of the Lord God that I am more than a conqueror through Him who loved me. I am not only a conqueror, but MORE than a conqueror through Him who loved me! I can do all things through Christ who strengthens me! I am strong! I am not weak—I am strong!

"I AM STRONG! I am strong in my spirit, my body, and my mind. I am strong financially. I am strong to do mighty exploits for God. I boldly confess before all I meet today that I am strong! Father

I rejoice in Your strength. I am strong in You, Lord, and in the power of Your might!

"Therefore, I banish every fear. I command weakness to leave me in all areas because it does not belong. It is the curse of the law, and it has nothing to do with me. I confess it with my mouth. Father, Your Word says that I can have whatever I say. I believe it right now, whether I feel it or not. I am strong in every area of my life. I rejoice in You, Lord, and in the power of Your might that exists in my body!

"Oh hallelujah! Father, I stand before you unafraid. I rejoice! I praise You! I thank You with all my heart that MY CONFESSION becomes MY POSSESSION. I am strong in the Lord and in the power of His might!

"I HAVE STRENGTH TO OVERCOME EVERY ATTACK OF SATAN."

6

A Confession of Prosperity and Victory

Nothing has given me more delight than confessing the Psalms before the Lord.

This confession is based on Psalm One. Read this wonderful Psalm right now. Meditate upon it, and let it sink into your spirit.

Now with it fresh in your heart, lift up your voice and make the following confession before the Lord. Make your confession several times daily. As you continually confess the Word of God, it will become your own. The truth of God's Word will sink into your heart, and your lips will begin to speak it out with great assurance.

Blessed is the man that walketh not in the counsel of the ungodly, nor standeth in the way of sinners, nor sitteth in the seat of the scornful. But his delight is in the law of the Lord; and in his law doth he meditate day and night. And he shall be like a tree planted by the rivers of water, that bringeth forth his fruit in his season; his leaf also shall not wither; and whatsoever he doeth shall prosper (Psalm 1:1-3).

CONFESSION OF PROSPERITY AND VICTORY

"Father, I come before You today with Your Word in my heart and upon my lips. I know the Bible says, *For verily I say unto you, That whosoever shall say unto this mountain, Be thou removed, and be thou cast into the sea; and shall not doubt in his heart, but shall believe that those things which he saith shall come to pass; he shall have whatsoever he saith* (Mark 11:23).

"I will not say that I am defeated and weak. I will not say that I am down, or that I have trouble and sorrow. I will not say that I cannot do the things that I have to do.

"Lord, today I will say what Your Words says. I dare to come before Your throne boldly, knowing that the Lord Jesus Christ is the High Priest of my confession.

"Lord, I put Your words in my mouth because I believe that Your Word is eternally settled in heaven (see Psalm 119:89). It is settled in my heart! I believe that Your Word is alive and powerful and sharper than any two-edged sword (see Hebrews 4:12). Lord, I believe that Your Word will never return to You void, but it shall prosper in the thing whereto You sent it (see Isaiah 55:11).

"Today, Lord, I take this blessed Psalm, which came from the lips of Your servant David, and I bring it to You. I make this Psalm my own, for it is the eternal Word of God. Therefore, I say: I am blessed. I am not cursed—I am blessed. I am not sad—I am happy. I am not filled with depression—I am filled with joy. I say that I am blessed. I am blessed in my home. I am blessed because I have health and strength. I am blessed, O Lord God, because I have Your promises.

"I am blessed because I walk not in the counsel of the ungodly. I stand not in the way of sinners, and I sit not in the seat of the scornful.

"THIS IS MY BOLD CONFESSION—

• I will counsel with godly people.

Your Word is my counselor. The Holy Ghost is my counselor, and the Lord Jesus is my counselor.

• I will not stand in the way of sinners.

I will not go to the places where sin abounds. I will not talk like sinners. I will not live like sinners. I am redeemed—I am a child of God.

• I will not sit in the seat of the scornful.

I will not be filled with unforgiveness. I will not be filled with jealousy or pride. I will not be filled with hatred or ill feelings. I will not be scornful toward life.

"I boldly declare that my delight is in the law of the Lord. My delight is not to do evil or to walk in the way of the world. My delight is not to fill my heart with the things of this world. My delight is not to fill my mind with the things of this world. My delight is in the law of the Lord! The Word of

God is the law of the Lord, and I meditate on it day and night.

"Lord, I take the great promises and truths of the Word of God, and I meditate upon them day and night. As I begin the day, drive my automobile, and go about the duties of the day, I meditate upon Your Word. When trouble arises, Lord, Your Word is within my heart. Even when I lie down at night in the last hours of the day, I meditate upon the great promises of God.

"The Word of God is my meditation day and night! *Let the words of my mouth, and the meditation of my heart, be acceptable in thy sight, O Lord, my strength, and my redeemer* (Psalm 19:14). Lord, because I meditate upon Your Word both day and night, I am like a tree. Your Word says that I am like a tree—therefore, I AM like a tree…not a little tree, but a big tree…not a weak tree, but a strong tree.

"I am like a tree planted by the rivers of water. My roots go down deep, Lord God, and reach the sustenance and the power of the water of Life that the world does not know anything about. I am like a tree planted by the rivers of water.

"I bring forth my fruit in its season. Lord, I declare that I am bringing forth fruit. I am a blessing to people today. I am winning souls and helping people today. I am encouraging people today. I am bringing forth fruit in my daily life.

"My leaf also shall not wither. Lord God, nothing in my life shall wither. I will not live a withered life. My life is filled with life and strength and the power of the Holy Ghost. My leaf shall not wither.

"I boldly declare that whatever I do shall prosper. I am not a failure. I boldly declare that I am not cast down in defeat, but whatever I do shall prosper. It does not matter what circumstances may look like. Lord God, I confess what Your Word says. I am prospering today—spiritually, physically, mentally, and financially. I am prospering in my marriage, and in every area of my life. I am living in prosperity because of the Word of the living God. Whatever I do shall prosper!

"Lord, I praise You that this is true. I boldly declare, confirm, and confess that this is true.

"I am like a tree growing by the rivers of water. My leaf also shall not wither, and whatever I do shall prosper. Oh hallelujah! Lord, I just praise You. I lift up my hands today and praise Your Name. I thank You that I am filled with Your love and Your joy. I thank You that I am prosperous in all that I do. I declare that whatever I do shall prosper. I call the things that be not as though they were (see Romans 4:17).

"I claim the first Psalm as my own today because it is the truth. No devil shall be able to stand before me all the days of my life.

"Lord, I know that You are with me and that You will never leave me nor forsake me. Just as You were with Moses, Joshua, Elijah, and the Lord Jesus Christ—I DECLARE THAT YOU ARE WITH ME.

"Lord, You commanded Joshua to be strong and of good courage. I like to meditate on the words You spoke to him because I know that You are speaking to me, also. *Only be thou strong and very courageous, that thou mayest observe to do according to all the law, which Moses my servant commanded thee: turn not from it to the right hand or to the left, that thou mayest prosper withersoever thou goest* (Joshua 1:7).

"Lord, I thank You that this is my confession: I am strong and of good courage. I am strong and very courageous. I observe to do Your law, the LAW OF LOVE.

"I will live in love and obey your commandments, Lord. I will obey Your law, and I will not turn from it to the right hand or to the left. I will prosper whithersoever I go. Lord, Psalm One says that whatever I do shall prosper. This means that wherever I go I shall prosper.

"I boldly declare, according to Joshua 1:8, *This book of the law shall not depart out of* [MY] *mouth, but* [I] *shall meditate therein day and night...*

"I will observe Your law and meditate in Your Word day and night. I thank You that whatever I do will prosper and wherever I go I will prosper. I thank You that I will make my way prosperous and have good success.

"Lord, have You not commanded me to be strong? I am strong and of good courage! I am not afraid nor dismayed!

"Lord, I am meditating in Your Word even now. I am confessing Your Word to You. I will not only confess Your Word, but I will observe to do it.

"Lord, I thank You that I am strong and of good courage. I am not afraid today of life, or death. I am not afraid of problems, circumstances, or people. I am not afraid of demons or the devil. I am not afraid of anything I face today. I am not dismayed or discouraged. WHY? Because, Lord God, You are with me whithersoever I go. You are the strength of my life.

"I AM BLESSED. Today I will rejoice and be a blessing to all I meet. I boldly make this confession. I believe it in my heart and confess it with my mouth. It is mine. It materializes because You, Lord, said that I can have whatsoever I say.

"I boldly declare that as I meet people and they ask me how I am, I will say, 'I am blessed!' I am blessed because I walk not in the counsel of the ungodly, nor stand in the way of sinners, nor sit in the seat of the scornful. I am blessed because my delight is in the law of the Lord, and in His law do I meditate day and night. Therefore, I am like a tree planted by the rivers of water. I do bring forth my fruit in its season. My leaf also shall not wither, and whatever I do shall prosper.

"I will have a good report for all I meet today. I will not talk of sickness and weakness. I will not talk of ill health and problems. I will talk as though God were with me, because He is with me. I will let those I meet today hear the joyful sound from my lips: 'I AM BLESSED! I AM BLESSED OF THE LORD MY GOD!' Father, I rejoice because these Words are eternally true and they are mine.

"I AM LIVING IN PROSPERITY AND VICTORY!"

7

A Confession of God's Abundant Supply

God wants to meet our needs. His desire is that we be at peace with Him and with ourselves. He wants us to be totally free from worry and fear.

Psalm Twenty-three is a beautiful expression of God's love for us. Meditate on these scriptures until you know in your spirit that God will take care of you and supply all of your needs.

Make the following confession with a thankful heart. Learn to praise and worship God because of His love for you.

The Lord is my shepherd; I shall not want. He maketh me to lie down in green pastures: he leadeth me beside the still waters. He restoreth my soul: he leadeth me in the paths of righteousness for his name's sake. Yea, though I walk through the valley of the shadow of death, I will fear no evil: for thou art with me; thy rod and thy staff they comfort me. Thou preparest a table before me in the presence of mine enemies: thou anointest my head with oil; my cup runneth over. Surely goodness and mercy shall follow me all the days of my life: and I will dwell in the house of the Lord for ever (Psalm 23).

CONFESSION OF GOD'S ABUNDANT SUPPLY

"Father, as I come to You today, I rejoice because I am Your child. I rejoice because You are my Father. I rejoice because Jesus is seated at Your right hand, ever living to make intercession for me.

"Father, Your Word says to come boldly to the throne of grace in order to obtain mercy and find grace to help in the time of need. Lord, I know that this is a time of need.

"You know every need I have in my spirit, mind, and physical body. You know every need I have materially and financially. You know every need I have in my family circle. You know every heartache and every burden that I bear.

"Lord, according to Your Word, I know that I shall have whatever I say. Many times the things that I have said—my wrong confessions—have brought destruction in my life.

"I have found a truth: IF I WILL CHANGE WHAT I SAY AND CONFESS YOUR WORD, I CAN CHANGE WHAT I HAVE.

"I will not confess what my body feels, what my eyes see, or what my senses tell me, but I will boldly confess Your Word, knowing that I shall have whatever I say.

"I take Psalm Twenty-three today and make it my own. I confess it at Your throne. I boldly declare that it is mine. Lord Jesus, You are my Shepherd. Yes, You are MY Shepherd. You said, *I am the good shepherd...* (John 10:14). The good shepherd gives His life for the sheep. I thank You because You are MY Shepherd. Yes, You are the Shepherd of the great family of God. I know that You are the Shepherd of thousands of people.

"Lord, You are the One who watches over me to feed me, guide me, and shield me. I boldly confess that You are not only my Lord and Savior, but You are my Shepherd. You are the One who watches over me when the world forgets me. There is One I know who looks down upon me. Your eyes never fail to follow me. Your love surrounds me because You love me so dearly.

"Lord, You see that I go the right way, that I am fed, and that I am shielded from evil. Lord Jesus, You are my Shepherd! Father, I am glad that You made Your Son my Shepherd. He will not fail. He will not fail ME! He will not fail to be a good Shepherd. He will not run off like a hireling and leave me to the wolves, but He will patiently and faithfully guard me and my family.

"Because You are my Shepherd, Lord Jesus, I boldly say, I DO NOT WANT! I do not lack. I do not have a care in this world. I do not have any anxiety today. I do not have one burden because I cast my burden upon the Lord. I bless Your Holy Name! Lord, You sustain me.

"I DO NOT WANT! I do not want, Lord, because You are supplying every need that I have. Has not Your Word said, *But my God shall supply all your need according to his riches in glory by Christ Jesus* (Philippians 4:19)? Has not Your Word said, *And ye are complete in him...* (Colossians 2:10)?

"Lord, I praise You today because You are my Shepherd, and You are faithfully taking care of me. I DO NOT WANT.

"Lord, you are supplying all I need spiritually, physically, financially, and materially. You are taking care of my family. You supply my every need.

"As my Shepherd, You have made me to lie down in green pastures. You are leading me beside the still waters. Lord, You are restoring my soul. You are leading me in the paths of righteousness for Your Name's sake.

"Lord Jesus, when I do not know where to go, I listen to You and follow You. I follow the path of love, joy, peace, longsuffering, gentleness, goodness, faith, meekness, temperance, wisdom, and understanding.

"I thank You, Lord, that You are leading me along the wonderful paths of forgiveness and tenderness toward all people. You are directing all of my ways.

"Father, I meditate on Your Word, which says, *Trust in the Lord with all thine heart; and lean not unto thine own understanding. In all thy ways acknowledge him, and he shall direct thy paths* (Proverbs 3:5-6).

"Lord, I thank You that You ARE directing my paths. I acknowledge, Lord, that I am just like a sheep. I do not know which way to turn many times, but I stay close to Jesus. As I read Your Word and meditate upon it, You lead me in the paths of righteousness for Your name's sake.

"YOU ARE MY GUIDE! You are my Shepherd, and I am following You daily. I am not afraid because everything that comes to me must pass You first. You know everything because You are in front of me, leading me all the way!

"I say with David, *Yea though I walk through the valley of the shadow of death, I will fear no evil.* Your Word did not say that I would stay in the valley, it said I would GO THROUGH!

"I boldly confess, Father, that I will fear no evil. I WILL FEAR NO EVIL! Why? Because You are with me, and Your rod and staff comfort me. Lord, it does not matter what I face now or in the future. If I go through the valley of the shadow of death...or have my heart broken...or go through sorrow and heartache...or face insurmountable circumstances and mountains of difficulties, I WILL FEAR NO EVIL! I will not fear because there stands beside me to lead, guide, direct, and shield me, THE LORD JESUS CHRIST.

"Lord, You are with me, and Your rod and staff comfort me. You prepare a table before me in the presence of my enemies—right in the presence of demonic powers, and even in the presence of Satan himself. You prepare a table, a banqueting table of victory, joy, and strength. Lord, I thank You that You prepare it right in the presence of my enemies.

"You anoint my head with oil. My cup runs over! Surely goodness and mercy shall follow me all the days of my life, and I will dwell in the house of the Lord forever!

"Lord this is my confession of victory! I am glad, Lord Jesus, that You are with me. I know that You will never leave me nor forsake me (see Hebrews 13:5). You are with me withersoever I go; therefore, NOTHING can overcome me...*because greater is he that is in* [me], *than he that is in the world* (1 John 4:4). The FATHER is in me. The SON is in me. The HOLY GHOST is in me. Oh Father, Son, and Holy Ghost, You are greater than any power of the enemy, and circumstances, or any problem. I am an overcomer!

"Lord, You will never leave me nor forsake me. Therefore, as I face life today, I face it fearlessly. I confidently put these words upon my lips. When people ask me today, "Well, how is it with you?" I will boldly say, 'The Lord is my Shepherd.' I do not have a want, a care, or any anxiety.

"God made me the salt of the earth, the light of the world, and the righteousness of God. Through Him, I am forgiven, delivered, and healed. I am more than a conqueror. I am blessed of the Lord.

"This is my joyful confession today. I will confess it before men and they, too, shall be lifted up and blessed. As they leave my presence, people will say, 'This one is surely blessed of the Lord.'

"Hallelujah! I praise You, Father, because I shall have whatever I say!

"GOD ABUNDANTLY SUPPLIES ALL MY NEEDS!"

8

A Confession of Victory Over Fear

Untold legions of demons have been turned loose on this generation. Demons of fear and torment are attacking many. Jesus said that in the last days, men's hearts would fail them for fear (see Luke 21:26). Fear is a tormenting spirit (see 1 John 4:18).

Read Psalm Ninety-one several times, and let it sink into your heart as you meditate upon it.

Make the confession with me. Surely no day should pass without you boldly knowing this confession so well that you can repeat it anytime and anywhere. God, by the power of His Word, will lift you to a plane of victory where every trace of fear and torment will be banished.

> *He that dwelleth in the secret place of the most High shall abide under the shadow of the Almighty. I will say of the Lord, He is my refuge* [protection or shelter from danger or hardship] *and my fortress* [a large and per-

manent stronghold]: *my God; in him will I trust. Surely he shall deliver thee from the snare of the fowler* [hunter], *and from the noisome pestilence* [fatal epidemics or evil influences]. *He shall cover thee with his feathers, and under his wings shalt thou trust: his truth shall be thy shield and buckler. Thou shalt not be afraid for the terror* [intense, overpowering fear] *by night; nor for the arrow* [the evil plots and slanders of the wicked] *that flieth by day; nor for the pestilence* [fatal epidemics or evil influences] *that walketh in darkness; nor for the destruction* [sudden death] *that wasteth at noonday.*

A thousand shall fall at thy side, and ten thousand at thy right hand; but it shall not come nigh thee. Only with thine eyes shalt thou behold and see the reward of the wicked. Because thou hast made the Lord, which is my refuge [protection or shelter from danger or hardship], *even the most High, thy habitation; there shall no evil befall thee, neither shall any plague* [affliction or calamity] *come nigh thy dwelling. For he shall give his angels charge over thee, to keep thee in all thy ways. They shall bear thee up in their hands, lest thou dash thy foot against a stone. Thou shalt tread upon the lion and adder: the young lion and the dragon shalt thou trample under feet. Because he hath set his love upon me, therefore will I deliver him: I will set him on high, because he hath known my name. He shall call upon me, and I will answer him: I will be with him in trouble; I will deliver him, and honour him. With long life will I satisfy him, and show him my salvation* (Psalm 91).

In the last three verses of this beautiful Psalm, God gives us seven promises. These promises are contingent upon one fact: that we set our love upon Him. When we love Him, He will deliver us and set us on high. He will answer us when we call upon Him and be with us in trouble, and He will honor us. He will satisfy us with long life and show us His salvation.

CONFESSION OF VICTORY OVER FEAR

"Oh Father, as I come to You today, I come with Your Word. I will not confess anything that is of the devil or of the world. I will not let pass from my lips that which would grieve You or harm me, but I will put Your words within my lips and confess them at Your great throne.

"I know that words can be destructive or they can be strength to those who walk uprightly. I choose to speak Your words, Father, because they are life. Your Word is eternally settled in heaven.

"God said to Joshua, the great deliverer, *This book of the law shall not depart out of thy MOUTH...* (Joshua 1:8).

"King David said, *I will SAY of the Lord...* (Psalm 91:2).

"The Word of the Lord came to the Prophet Jeremiah—*Is not my word like as a fire? saith the Lord; and like a hammer that breaketh the rock in pieces?* (Jeremiah 23:29).

"Mary, the mother of Jesus, said, ...*be it unto me according to thy word* (Luke 1:38).

"Therefore, I say, let it be unto me according to Your Word. I take Your Word and not only put it in my heart, but I speak it with my mouth. I confess this Psalm to You today. I confess that I dwell in the secret place of the Most High. I abide under the shadow of the Almighty. Lord, this is my dwelling place! It is not where I visit once in awhile. I declare that I dwell in the secret place of the Most High.

"I thank You, Father, that in this wicked world in which I live, there is a secret place—a hiding place under the shadow of Your wings. Lord, that hiding place is in Your presence. Wherever I go, I can sense Your divine presence. I can sense the divine influence of Your Spirit upon my life. So I can boldly say: I dwell in the secret place of the Most High. I abide under the shadow of the Almighty.

"Oh Father, I am glad You are close to me. In You I live and move and have my being. Lord Jesus, You said that You would never leave me nor forsake me. Lord, You said You would send another Comforter, the Holy Spirit, who will abide with me forever.

"My body is the temple of the Holy Ghost. I am not my own. I belong to God. I am bought with a price. Therefore, I glorify God in my body and in my spirit, which are His (see 1 Corinthians 6:19-20). I thank You, Lord God, that You said You will walk in me and You will be my God and I will be Your child. The greater One lives within me. I dwell in the secret place of the Most High. I abide under the shadow of the Almighty. This is my living place!

"Some people ask me, 'Where do you live?' and I could give them the address of my house— but, Father, I really live in the secret place of the Most High! I abide under the shadow of the Almighty! In the midst of all the storms of life, all the confusion of life, all the turbulence of life, and all the troubles of life, I AM ABIDING UNDER THE SHADOW OF THE ALMIGHTY.

"And what shall I say of the Lord? What shall be upon my lips about the Lord today? Shall I say the Lord has failed me...I do not understand the Lord...or the Lord has brought sickness and sorrow and trouble upon me?

"No! I will not make the enemy happy by saying things such as these! What shall I say of the Lord? I will say what God's Word says. The Lord is my refuge and my fortress. The Lord is my God; in Him will I trust.

"Oh Father, this is what I say about You. Lord Jesus, this is what I say about You: You are my refuge and my fortress. You are my God—the One I trust.

"Surely You have delivered me from the snare of the fowler and from the noisome pestilence. You have covered me with Your feathers and under Your wings I trust. Your truth is my shield and my buckler. Hallelujah! This is my confession about the Lord.

"I will not have a negative confession and talk about my trouble, my sorrow, and all the things I do not understand. Lord, I boldly confess that You are my refuge, my fortress, my God! Your truth is my shield and my buckler. You have delivered me from the snare of the fowler. You have delivered me from the noisome pestilence. You have covered me with Your feathers, and under Your wings I trust.

"Lord God, Your truth is what I am confessing today. I live in Your Word. I read it daily and meditate upon it. I speak it out to men, and I confess it to You. The Word of the Lord endures forever! No Word of God shall be void of power. Your Word, Father, is truth. Every Word of God is inspired by the Holy Spirit, and it...*is profitable for doctrine, for reproof, for correction, for instruction in righteousness: that the man* [or woman] *of God may be perfect, thoroughly furnished unto all good works* (2 Timothy 3:16-17).

"Lord, I thank You that I have overcome the devil by the blood of the Lamb and the word of my testimony. Your Word is my testimony today. Your truth is my shield and my buckler, therefore, I say I AM NOT AFRAID!

"Father, it is said that in the last days men's hearts will fail them because of fear. I know that fear has been let loose upon the human race, but I boldly confess that I am not afraid! I am not afraid of fear! I am not afraid of the devil or demons. I am not afraid of sickness, cancer, or an early death. I am not afraid of divorce! I am not afraid that my children will go astray! I am not afraid that the members of my family will never be saved! I am not afraid that I have committed the unpardonable sin! I am not afraid that God does not love me! I am not afraid of trouble, sorrow, and heartache! I AM NOT AFRAID!

"Lord, I confess that I am bold and courageous. I am a strong person—a mighty soldier of the Lord Jesus Christ. I stand up tall and square my shoulders. I am a bold soldier of the Lord Jesus Christ, and I am not afraid! I want the devil to hear this—Devil, I am not afraid! I want the angels to hear it—Angels, I am not afraid! I want the Lord Jesus to hear it—Jesus, I am not afraid! Father, I want You to hear it—I am not afraid! I am not afraid, Lord, because You will never leave me nor forsake me. I HAVE NO FEAR! I refuse fear in my spirit, mind, and body. I AM NOT AFRAID!

"As I read this Psalm, Lord, I see what I am not afraid of. I am not afraid of the terror by night. I will not give in to intense, overpowering fear. I am not afraid of the arrow that flies by day or of the evil plots and slanders of the wicked. I am not afraid of the pestilence that walks in darkness. I do not fear any fatal epidemic or evil influence. I am not afraid of the destruction that wastes at noonday. I am not afraid of sudden death.

"Lord, I am not afraid of any of the devil's schemes. I am not afraid of what is going to happen in the morning or during the day. I am not afraid of what is going to happen at noontime or during the night. I AM NOT AFRAID!

"I am not afraid because God is my Father, and if He is for me, who can be against me? Lord Jesus, You are my Lord and my Savior. The Holy Spirit dwells within me, and I am surrounded by the angels of God. I AM NOT AFRAID!

"I am going to stop and praise You with uplifted hands. Hallelujah! Hallelujah! I praise You, Lord. I am delivered from fear. I do not care if I feel fear or not. I am not afraid of it. I am not afraid of fear. I will not entertain fear. When fear comes against my mind, I hold up the blood of Jesus and cry, 'THE BLOOD! THE BLOOD! THE BLOOD! Satan, the blood of the Lord Jesus Christ is against You!' Then those evil imaginations disappear! I realize that my God is able to deliver me out of ALL of the troubles of life!

"I AM NOT AFRAID! I boldly declare it...I believe it in my heart...and I confess it with my mouth. All fear has to leave me. I command you, you spirits of fear, in the Name of Jesus and in the power of the blood of Jesus, to leave me now! Get away from me! Get out of this room! Get out of this house! Get away from all of my family! Leave now, you spirits of fear! I am not afraid. I have all power over all demonic forces in the Name of the Lord Jesus Christ (see Luke 10:19). I command you to leave me! Flee from me according to the Word of God!

"Father, You have not given me the spirit of fear, but the spirit of power and of love and of a sound mind (see 2 Timothy 1:7). I boldly confess that I do not have the spirit of fear, for the spirit of fear has fled from me according to Your Word, which says, …*Resist the devil, and he will flee from you* (James 4:7).

"I boldly declare that I have the spirit of love, power, and a sound mind. I am filled with love, power, and a sound mind by Your Spirit. A thousand may fall at my side and ten thousand at my right hand, but it shall not come near me. Only with my eyes shall I behold and see the reward of the wicked.

"Now, the devil would tell me that I am going to fail, my family is going to be destroyed, and tragedy is going to come. But I say boldly, 'Lord, a thousand may fall at my side and ten thousand at my right hand, but it shall not come near me!' This is the Word of the eternal God, and I boldly declare that it is true! NO EVIL SHALL COME NEAR ME!

"Only with my eyes shall I see the reward of the wicked. Father, demonic forces lined against me shall be rewarded with everlasting destruction from the Lord. They are eternally defeated, for Jesus spoiled principalities and powers and made a show of them openly, triumphing over them (see Colossians 2:15). He was manifested to destroy the works of the devil (see 1 John 3:8).

"Now, Father, I come to the reward of such a confession. Because I have made the Lord my habitation, my dwelling place, and my portion, there shall no evil befall me, neither shall any plague or calamity come near my dwelling. I boldly confess that no evil shall befall me. No plague or calamity shall come near my dwelling.

"Lord, this is my confession because You have given Your angels charge over me to keep me in all my ways. They will bear me up in their hands lest I dash my foot against a stone. Father, Your angels accompany me, defend me, and preserve me. Thank You, Lord, for those blessed ministering spirits. Even though I do not see them, they are busy at work every hour of the day, watching over me and my loved ones.

"I boldly confess that I tread upon the lion and the adder, and the young lion and the dragon I trample under foot. Because I have set my love upon You, Lord, You will deliver me and set me on high. You will answer me when I call upon You, and You will be with me in trouble. You will honor me, satisfy me with long life, and show me Your salvation. This is true in my life. You have answered me when I have called upon You. You are with me in trouble. You have not deserted me, but You have delivered me. You are honoring me daily with Your presence, Your power, Your mercy, and Your goodness.

"Lord, you will satisfy me with long life, and the number of my days You will fulfill (see Exodus 23:26).

"Because I serve You, Lord, You have blessed my bread and my water. You have taken sickness from the midst of me. I boldly confess today that You will satisfy me with long life. I will not die an early death. Sickness will not take my life from me because You have taken sickness from the midst of me. The number of my days You will fulfill. I thank You, Father, that You are all powerful. There is no power so great as that of my Heavenly Father!

"Father, I confidently rejoice in You because You are the preserver of my life. You are the strength of my life. You are the God of this universe, and You are my very own Father! I do not fear or fret! I do not have any anxiety today! You are my Father! Lord Jesus, You are my Shepherd! The Holy Spirit is my mighty Teacher and Comforter! The angels of God are about me! I have been washed in the blood of Jesus, and I am a child of God!

"Today, I am full of love, joy, peace, and power.

"Father, today I will share the Good News with those around me. I will not have an evil report, but I will have a good report. No words shall pass my lips except that which pertains to Your Word. This is my confession. I praise You, Father, because You are watching over Your Word to see that it is fulfilled in my life (see Jeremiah 1:12).

"I HAVE VICTORY OVER FEAR!"

9

A Confession of What Jesus Is to Me

The following confession will change what you believe about yourself. Take time to meditate on Psalm Twenty-seven. As you read and confess it aloud day after day, you will suddenly know that the Lord IS your light and salvation. You will know that you have nothing to fear because He is the strength of your life.

The Lord is my light and my salvation; whom shall I fear? the Lord is the strength of my life; of whom shall I be afraid? When the wicked, even mine enemies and my foes, came upon me to eat up my flesh, they stumbled and fell. Though an host should encamp against me, my heart shall not fear: though war should rise against me, in this will I be confident. One thing have I desired of the Lord, that will I seek after; that I may dwell in the house of the Lord all the days of my life, to behold the beauty of the Lord, and to inquire in his temple. For in the time of trouble he shall hide me in his pavilion: in the secret of his tabernacle shall he hide me; he shall set me up upon a rock. And now shall mine head be lifted up above mine enemies round about me: therefore will I offer in his tabernacle sacrifices of joy; I will sing, yea, I will sing praises unto the Lord (Psalm 27:1-6).

A CONFESSION OF WHAT JESUS IS TO ME

"Father, I come to Your throne today, rejoicing that I am a Christian and that I am washed in the blood of the Lamb of God. I am rejoicing that I am a new creature in Christ Jesus and that You are my very own Father and I am Your very own child.

"Lord, as I approach Your great and wonderful throne, I will turn to You, confess Your Word, and have whatever I say. As I approach Your throne, confessing Psalm Twenty-seven, it will not be written words only, but it shall become living words to me because I claim it as my own.

"You said, in Deuteronomy 11:24, *Every place whereon the soles of your feet shall tread shall be yours....* Today I put the soles of my feet as if they were on Psalm Twenty-seven, and I claim that land as my own. Father, I boldly confess Your Word and declare that these great truths are mine.

"I say with King David, Lord, You are my light and my salvation; who shall I fear? Lord, You are the strength of my life; of whom shall I be afraid? Oh my Father, I praise You because the Lord Jesus is the light of the world. Jesus said to me, *Ye are the light of the world...* (Matthew 5:14). I thank You, Lord Jesus, that You are my light! I will not walk in darkness because I know the Light of life. I will not be afraid of the darkness of this generation. I will not be afraid of the darkness that is coming upon the land. I thank You, O Lord, that You are my light.

"Jesus, You live on the inside of me, and You are my salvation. Salvation is forgiveness, healing, deliverance, wholeness, health, peace, and rest. Jesus, You are my salvation. You are all I will ever need to be free from the power of the enemy. You are my salvation. I flee unto the rock that is higher than I am. You are that rock. You are my light and my salvation. In You are hidden all the treasures of the wisdom and knowledge of God (see Colossians 2:3). Lord Jesus, I am complete in You.

"You are my light and my salvation. You are the strength of my life. You live on the inside of me, and You are my strength. Your strength is my strength. Lord God, today I can boldly say that I have light, health, and strength. I have the Lord Jesus Christ!

"I am in Christ, and Christ is in me! Oh Father...I praise You for Your Son. Lord Jesus, You said if any man serve You, him will Your Father honor. Father, You have honored me with life, strength, and salvation both day and night. I am so glad that I walk in the blessings of God.

"Lord, I thank You that You are my light and my salvation. You are the strength of my life, and I am not afraid. If God is for me, who can be against me? (see Romans 8:31).

"Lord God, You are my Father. Jesus, You are my Lord. The Holy Spirit is my comforter, helper, and strengthener. Therefore, I am not afraid of anyone or anything. I AM NOT AFRAID! I fear not! I am not dismayed because the Lord my God is with me wherever I go.

"Lord, I praise You today because You are my light and my salvation, and I am not afraid. When the wicked, even mine enemies and my foes, come upon me to eat up my flesh, they stumble and fall. This is my confession today. When demonic powers come against me mentally, spiritually, physically, emotionally, and maritally, THEY STUMBLE AND FALL!

"I am covered by the blood of the Lord Jesus Christ, and that blood is a hedge about me. No devil or demon power can cross that hedge. They must stumble and fall. Lord, I am not afraid because You have a hedge about me. The blood of the Lord Jesus Christ is over me, and the angel of the Lord encamps round about me. Goodness and mercy follow me, and the Lord goes before me. Underneath me are Your everlasting arms.

"Lord, You have made me to KNOW that when my enemies come against me, they will stumble and fall. Though an host encamp against me, my heart will not fear.

"I desire one thing, Lord, and this will I seek after—that I may dwell in the house of the Lord all the days of my life to behold the beauty of the Lord, and to inquire in His holy temple.

"Lord, I have confidence in You because I desire, more than anything else in the world, to dwell in the secret place of the Most High, to have a relationship with You, to behold the beauty of the Lord, and to live in the presence of the Lord.

"In the time of trouble, Father, You hide me in Your pavilion. In the secret of Your tabernacle, You hide me and set me upon a rock. I know that we all will have trouble because those who live godly in Christ Jesus shall suffer persecution. Trouble comes to all, but I boldly confess that in the time of trouble, You hide me. You hide me from the devil and demon powers. You hide me under the blood of the Lord Jesus Christ. You hide me, Lord God, in Your pavilion, in the secret of Your tabernacle. You set me upon a rock.

"That rock is the Lord Jesus Christ, and He is high above all of my enemies where they cannot reach me. So I say with the psalmist that my head is now lifted up above my enemies round about me. Oh yes, I am lifted up!

"I am more than a conqueror through the Lord Jesus Christ. I am set upon the rock, and I will not be shaken. I will not be defeated, for greater is He that is in me than he that is in the world. Therefore, I say with King David, I will offer in Your tabernacle sacrifices of joy. I will sing, yea, I will sing praises unto the Lord. I am not going to moan and groan and complain today. I offer sacrifices of joy and sing praises unto the Lord. Hallelujah! Praise the Lord! Blessed be the Name of the Lord!

"Father, I bless Your holy Name today. I rejoice because Christ Jesus is my victory! He is my great Conqueror and He lives within me. Blessed be the Name of the Lord! I run through a troop and leap over a wall by the Name of the Lord, my God. I have overcome by the power of His Name today.

"Father, this is my confession today. I rejoice and praise You today. I thank You, Lord, that You are my light and my salvation. I am not afraid. This is my bold confession as I face life today with all of its problems, with all of its heartaches, with all the things that would engulf me with despair.

"I will not look at my circumstances. I will not dwell upon my situation, Lord, but I will say boldly and confidently these things about You. I will rejoice that these truths are actually becoming a part of my life. I believe them within my heart. I confess them with my mouth, and they are indeed made mine daily because the Bible says I shall have whatever I say.

"I rejoice that Psalm Twenty-seven is mine today. I will meditate upon it, confess it, talk about it, and rejoice that it is mine.

"JESUS IS MY LIGHT AND MY SALVATION!"

BOOKS BY JOHN OSTEEN

*A Miracle For Your Marriage
*A Place Called There
*ABC's of Faith
*Believing God For Your Loved Ones
  Deception! Recognizing True and False Ministries
  Four Principles in Receiving From God.
*Healed of Cancer by Dodie Osteen
*How To Claim the Benefits of the Will
*How To Demonstrate Satan's Defeat
  How To Flow in the Super Supernatural
  How To Minister Healing to the Sick
*How To Receive Life Eternal
  How To Release the Power of God
  Keep What God Gives
*Love & Marriage
  Overcoming Hindrances To Receiving the Baptism in the Holy Spirit
*Overcoming Opposition: How To Succeed in Doing the Will of God
    by Lisa Comes
*Pulling Down Strongholds
*Receive the Holy Spirit
  Reigning in Life as a King
  Rivers of Living Water
  Saturday's Coming
  Seven Facts About Prevailing Prayer
  Seven Qualities of a Man of Faith
*Six Lies the Devil Uses To Destroy Marriages by Lisa Comes
  Spiritual Food For Victorious Living
*The Believer's #1 Need
  The Bible Way to Spiritual Power
  The Confessions of a Baptist Preacher
*The Divine Flow
*The 6th Sense...Faith
  The Truth Shall Set You Free
*There Is a Miracle in Your Mouth
  This Awakening Generation
  Unraveling the Mystery of the Blood Covenant
*What To Do When Nothing Seems To Work
*What To Do When the Tempter Comes
  You Can Change Your Destiny

*Also available in Spanish.

Please write for a complete list of prices in the John Osteen Library.
Lakewood Church • P.O. Box 23297 • Houston, Texas 77228